FIRST-TIME FATHER FUNDAMENTALS:

A NEW DAD'S GUIDE TO NAVIGATING PREGNANCY, MANAGING DELIVERY ROOM EXPECTATIONS, AND MASTERING KEY PARENTING SKILLS

COLLIN WEBB

Copyright © 2024 by Collin Webb

All rights reserved.

No portion of this book may be reproduced in any form without written permission from the publisher or author, except as permitted by U.S. copyright law.

This publication is designed to provide accurate and authoritative information in regard to the subject matter covered. It is sold with the understanding that neither the author nor the publisher is engaged in rendering legal, investment, accounting or other professional services. While the publisher and author have used their best efforts in preparing this book, they make no representations or warranties with respect to the accuracy or completeness of the contents of this book and specifically disclaim any implied warranties of merchantability or fitness for a particular purpose. No warranty may be created or extended by sales representatives or written sales materials. The advice and strategies contained herein may not be suitable for your situation. You should consult with a professional when appropriate. Neither the publisher nor the author shall be liable for any loss of profit or any other commercial damages, including but not limited to special, incidental, consequential, personal, or other damages.

TABLE OF CONTENTS

Introduction	11
1. THE EMOTIONAL UPS AND DOWNS	13
1.1 From Panic to Excitement: Riding the Emotional Waves	14
1.2 Tackling the Fear of the Unknown Together	16
1.3 Balancing Joy and Anxiety: A Father's Mindset Shift	17
2. HORMONE HARMONY: *Emotional Support Strategies*	21
2.1 Mastering the Art of Pregnancy Empathy	21
2.2 Effective Communication During Hormonal Shifts	23
3. BUMP AND RUN: *The First Trimester*	27
3.1 Weeks 1-3: Ready, Set, Grow	27
3.2 Week 4: Seeing Double...Lines	29
3.3 Week 5: Tiny Tenant	30
3.4 Week 6: Feel the Rhythm	32
3.5 Week 7: From Blob to Babe	33
3.6 Week 8: Limbs in the Limelight	34
3.7 Week 9: Peek-a-Boo! I See You	35
3.8 Week 10: Leveling Up in the Womb	37
3.9 Week 11: Here Comes the Bump	38
3.10 Week 12: Fueling the Bump	39
4. BANKROLLING BABY: *Pennies, Pacifiers, and Plans*	41
4.1 Budgeting for Baby: A Realistic Guide	42
4.2 Insurance and Healthcare: Navigating the Maze	45
4.3 Saving for the Future: Education and Emergency Funds	46
4.4 Cost-Saving Tips for Expectant Fathers	48

5. GROWING AND GLOWING: 51
The 2nd Trimester

5.1 Week 13: Baby's Bigger, Better Sequel 51
5.2 Week 14: Mile-a-Minute Changes 52
5.3 Week 15: Kickoff Time 53
5.4 Week 16: Sensory Overload 55
5.5 Week 17: Insulation Installation 56
5.6 Week 18: Soundcheck 57
5.7 Week 19: Coating Baby in Comfort 58
5.8 Week 20: Halftime Show 59
5.9 Week 21: Gut Feelings 60
5.10 Week 22: Gestational Gymnastics 61
5.11 Week 23: Bloodline Begins 62
5.12 Week 24: Breath of Life 63
5.13 Week 25: Feeling the Feedback 64
5.14 Week 26: Eyes on the Prize 65
5.15 Week 27: Grey Matter Matters 66

6. THE PUSH PLAYBOOK: 69
Strategies for a Smooth Delivery

6.1 Choosing the Right Birth Plan for Your Family 70
6.2 Understanding the Role of Healthcare Professionals 73
6.3 Packing the Hospital Bag: A Dad's Checklist 75

7. NURSERY KNOW-HOW: 79
Dad's Guide to Essential Baby Gear

7.1 Setting Up the Nursery: A Dad's Checklist 79
7.2 Must-Have Gear for the First Six Months 82

8. FROM BUMP TO BABY: 89
3rd Trimester

8.1 Week 28: Butterball Baby 89
8.2 Week 29: The Great Stretch 90
8.3 Week 30: Shake, Rattle, and Roll 91
8.4 Week 31: Sense-sational Baby 93
8.5 Week 32: Snug as a Bug 94
8.6 Week 33: Building Baby's Immune Fort 95
8.7 Week 34: Fat Fortress 96
8.8 Week 35: Baby Bulk 97
8.9 Week 36: Breath of Fresh Air 98
8.10 Week 37: Lock and Load 99

8.11 Week 38: Ready to Roll	100
8.12 Week 39: Any Day Now	101
8.13 Week 40: It's Go Time!	102
8.14 Week 41: Overtime	103
8.15 Week 42: Eviction Notice	104

9. DAD'S DELIVERY DUTIES: 107
Delivery Room 101

9.1 Understanding the Stages of Labor from a Dad's Perspective	107
9.2 Essential Support Roles During Delivery	109
9.3 Understanding Different Birthing Scenarios and Interventions	111
9.4 Bonding with Your Baby: The First Touch	114

10. BABY BASICS: 115
A Dad's Guide to Newborns

10.1 Diaper Changing 101: Tips and Tricks	115
10.2 Understanding Newborn Sleep Patterns	118
10.3 Soothing Techniques and Handling a Fussy Baby	120
10.4 Splish Splash: The Basics of Baby Bathing	123
10.5 Bottle Feeding Basics for Dads	125
10.6 Supporting Breastfeeding: A Dad's Role	128

11. LITTLE LEAPS 131

11.1 The First 3 Months: What to Expect	131
11.2 4-6 Months: Encouraging Growth Through Play	133

12. BABY BLUES AND DADDY DO'S: 137
A Guide for Postpartum Care

12.1 Recognizing Signs of Postpartum Depression	137
12.2 Practical Ways to Support Physical Recovery	140
12.3 Recognizing and Managing Your Own Mental Health as a New Father	142

13. SHOTS AND TOTS: 145
Baby's Health Journey

13.1 Navigating Vaccination Decisions	145
13.2 Vaccination Schedule and Health Check-Ups	147
13.3 Home Safety for Crawlers and Walkers	149

14. ROMANCE AND RATTLES: 153
Balancing Love and Parenting
   14.1 Keeping the Spark Alive: Date Nights Post-Baby 154
   14.2 Communication and Teamwork in Parenting 156

Conclusion 159
References 161

To Heather,

My rock, my confidant, and my greatest love. This journey and every step in it I've taken are all because of your unwavering support and boundless love. Your strength and kindness inspire me every day. Thank you for standing by my side and for being an incredible mother to our children. Your nurturing spirit, endless patience, and unwavering devotion have created a home filled with love and laughter.

To Adam and Lily,

Discovering the world through your eyes and watching you grow fills me with immeasurable love, pride, and boundless hope for the future. Every laugh, every hug, and every shared moment is a treasure. May you always feel the depth of my love, and carry with you the lessons and love your mother and I strive to give you every day. This book is also for you, as a testament to the journey of fatherhood that you make so incredibly worthwhile.

"A father is neither an anchor to hold us back, nor a sail to take us there, but a guiding light whose love shows us the way."

UNKNOWN

INTRODUCTION

So, there you are, comfortably lounging on the couch, maybe even enjoying your favorite show. Then, your partner walks in, holding a tiny plastic stick with a look that says everything. You're going to be a Dad. Congratulations! Welcome to the whirlwind where baby cries are your new soundtrack, sleep becomes an elusive dream, and Google becomes your late-night confidant. Strap in—this wild ride is packed with ups and downs, laughs and screams, and plenty of tears (mostly the baby's), but it's sure to be your biggest adventure ever.

"First-Time Father Fundamentals" is not another book about being a dad. This is the guide you'll be referring to week after week. It's designed for guys like you who know how to draft the perfect fantasy football team but need help figuring out what to do in the baby aisle. Think of it as your road map through each trimester, the delivery room, and the first months of your child's life, with a bit of humor to keep things in perspective.

What can you expect from this guidebook? I've structured it into sections, each dedicated to a specific stage of the parenting journey.

We've got you covered, from preparing for your partner's pregnancy to managing the first poo-pacolypse. Each section is packed with practical advice, key developmental milestones, and strategies to support your baby and your partner.

I'm a proud veteran and a tech geek, both of which have taught me a thing or two about problem-solving and rolling with the punches. With two kids of my own, I've navigated midnight meltdowns and diaper disasters, emerging with a wealth of advice and a collection of stories. I've distilled all this knowledge and a relentless drive to simplify the complex into the pages of this guidebook.

You're probably excited and scared out of your mind about the idea of fatherhood. But I'm here to tell you, you can do it. This book will give you the confidence and knowledge to handle everything from diaper duty to bedtime battles.

And it's not just a bunch of clichés. We'll talk about budgeting without boring you to tears, tackle co-parenting like a pro, and even how to keep the romance alive. And I promise you'll smile along the way. We will keep things light, relatable, and real so you can feel prepared and at ease as you embark on this journey.

So, consider this your invitation to take this journey with me. By the end of this book, you'll be ready for the practical side of parenting and excited about the adventure of raising a tiny human.

Get ready, future dad. Open your mind, get ready to learn and laugh, and step confidently into fatherhood. Remember, you're not alone in this. I'm here to support you every step of the way. Let's do this together!

CHAPTER 1
THE EMOTIONAL UPS AND DOWNS

Have you ever watched one of those rollercoaster rides where people scream, laugh, and maybe get a little sick all at once? That's what finding out you're going to be a dad is like, except it lasts for months, and instead of ending up back where you started, you end up with a baby. It's a wild ride from "What?" to "I can do this!" but you're not alone. Every Dad-to-Be gets a ticket, and this chapter is here to help you through the ups, downs, and loop-de-loops.

1.1 FROM PANIC TO EXCITEMENT: RIDING THE EMOTIONAL WAVES

When I first heard the news that I would be a dad, it was delivered in a way I'll never forget. I came home one evening to find a neatly folded shirt on the bed that said "Every Hero Needs a Sidekick" and, next to it, a tiny baby onesie emblazoned with "Lil' Sidekick." A whirlwind of emotions swept through me—fear, excitement, disbelief. I stood there, holding the onesie; with my mind racing a mile a minute, I almost forgot to hug my wife. At that moment, I knew my life was about to change in the most incredible way.

The moment you find out you're going to be a father, it can be a lot to take in. Disbelief, joy, fear, and excitement—a cocktail that can bewilder any man. It's normal to feel like you've just been called to the major leagues after playing in your backyard. It's not a sign you're not ready to be a father; it's a sign you're human. In fact, it's a sign of just how significant this change is. Whether you're the kind of person who keeps to himself or wants to tell the world, it's all part of being a Dad-to-Be.

Dealing with this whirlwind might feel like putting together a crib without instructions. It's frustrating and a little overwhelming. The key here is to give yourself space and time to process. It's okay not to have all the answers or emotions figured out in one go. Break down your tasks and feelings into more manageable parts. For example, if the financial aspects of parenting concern you, you could start by looking up baby budgeting or attending a new-dad finance workshop. If you tackle each issue individually, you'll go from panicking to planning to even being excited. It's like building a tower of diapers; if you take it one step at a time, it won't fall over.

Communication with your partner during this time is more than good—it's necessary. You might think it's better to be the strong, silent type, but this isn't a silent movie. Talk about your fears, your excitement, and your confusion. This will not only help you and your partner, but it will also prepare you for co-parenting. Just a simple "Hey, I'm nervous about the delivery day. How do you feel?" can open up all kinds of conversations. And don't just talk to your partner; listen to them too. This back-and-forth can be your lifeline during this time.

While your partner is your copilot on this adventure, remember to lean on others for support. Whether it's your friends, family, or other dads who have been through the gauntlet of diapers and 2 AM feedings, these veterans can provide practical advice, emotional support, or even a good joke or two. You may be surprised to find that despite their tough-guy facades, other dads have gone through the same emotional rollercoaster and have some insights that can put your mind at ease. Consider finding a local or online dad group. Sharing your experiences with others can be incredibly reassuring and helpful.

Finally, let's talk about expectations—setting realistic ones is like putting guardrails on your rollercoaster. No parent, no matter how experienced, has all the answers. Parenting is not about being perfect. It's about trying, failing, and trying again. You and your partner will both need to adjust to new roles and new responsibilities. And you will need to be patient with one another. Parenthood is one of the most rigorous but rewarding roles you'll ever undertake, and setting realistic expectations for yourself and your partner will make this ride much smoother.

Becoming a dad is an emotional rollercoaster, but with the right tools and mindset, you can get through this with most of your sanity intact. You'll be thrilled one minute and terrified the next, but that's just the way it is. So hold on tight and get ready for the ride of your life.

1.2 TACKLING THE FEAR OF THE UNKNOWN TOGETHER

Let's get honest about those fears. There's the fear of not being a good enough dad, the financial stress of adding a new member to the family, and the fear of actually delivering your child without passing out. Then there's the biggest fear: handling a fragile newborn who seems to come with more instructions than that IKEA dresser you never quite finished assembling. These fears are not just expected; they're a universal rite of passage for every new dad.

So, how do you overcome them? First, you have to understand that you're not alone in this. Educate yourself about what you're about to face. I don't just mean the fun stuff like picking out a crib or decorating a nursery. You must know what to expect in the delivery room and what to do once the baby is born. The more you know, the less scary it all becomes. Knowing what's going on during labor will significantly help your partner.

Communication is your copilot in this journey. Talk to your partner about your fears. Odds are, she's just as scared as you are, and you both need to be strong for each other. Discuss everything from who'll change the diapers at 3 AM to how you'll handle visits from well-meaning but exhausting in-laws. These conversations can turn your individual fears into a shared battle plan.

You also need to prepare. This means more than just packing a hospital bag. It means getting your mind and body ready for what's to come. Go to some classes together, or practice putting in the car seat. Everything you do to prepare will make you a better dad and give you more confidence.

Finally, start planning for the future. Start thinking about what kind of dad you want to be. Whether planning a trip for the three of you or just imagining what it will be like to read bedtime stories, it helps to look forward to the future. And do it together. Make decisions as a couple, and you'll be better prepared for whatever comes your way.

It's also about teamwork. Going through pregnancy and parenthood with your partner can strengthen your relationship and provide a support system. Whether choosing the nursery's color or selecting a pediatrician, make these decisions together. Every decision you make as a team will only strengthen your relationship and your readiness to take on parenting.

And remember, the fear you feel is a sign of the great responsibility you are about to take on. Facing those fears doesn't just prepare you for fatherhood; with every challenge you conquer, every fear you overcome, and every plan you make, you are one step closer to being the father you want to be. So, take those fears and use them to your advantage.

1.3 BALANCING JOY AND ANXIETY: A FATHER'S MINDSET SHIFT

Imagine juggling. In one hand, you've got a bowling ball named Joy, and the other, a chainsaw named Anxiety—still running. Sounds like a circus trick gone wrong, right? But here's the thing: that's pretty much what it feels like navigating the emotional landscape of impending fatherhood. You're excited to meet the little guy or gal but terrified of the responsibility. It's pretty standard for men to feel both of these emotions simultaneously. Welcome to the dad club, where it feels like you're riding an emotional seesaw. It's all part of the initiation.

You don't need to become a Zen master to balance these emotions. It's more about understanding that it's okay to be excited about playing peek-a-boo or picking out the cutest onesies but also be worried about college funds and keeping the baby healthy. The key is not to let the anxiety outweigh the joy. For every concern you have, counter it with a positive thought. It's all about ensuring both sides of the seesaw are equal so you don't tip over.

Now, let's talk about mindfulness and presence. Before you think about sitting cross-legged and humming "Om," let me explain. Mindfulness isn't just for yogis; it's a practical tool for anyone who wants to reduce stress. It's about being present in the moment rather than worrying about the future. Start simple. Try focusing on your breathing for a few minutes each day, or take notice of your food when you eat—savor each bite, notice the textures and flavors. This isn't just about reducing stress; it's about enhancing your ability to enjoy the present moment, which will be incredibly beneficial when the baby arrives. It will allow you to enjoy those first smiles, the softness of your baby's hair, and even the midnight cries. It's all part of being a dad.

Adopting a positive outlook might sound like a cheesy motivational poster with a kitten hanging from a branch and the words "Hang in there!" But stick with me. Looking at the challenges and changes through a positive lens doesn't mean ignoring the hard parts; it means framing them in a way that makes them seem surmountable and even beneficial. Remember, every diaper change, every sleepless night, and even every time your baby spits up is building your resilience and capability as a father. Plus, let's face it, overcoming challenges can bring some of the greatest joys—like when you finally figure out how to swaddle your baby so they look like a burrito and sleep like an angel.

Finally, finding joy in the small moments can change the entire experience of pregnancy and early fatherhood from something anxiety-inducing to something beautiful. It's the small things—like the first time you felt your baby kick or seeing your partner light up when they talk about what color they want to paint the nursery. It's easy to forget about these moments, but they're the highlights amid the chaos. They're what remind you of the amazing journey you are on together. So make sure to look for these small joys every day. It could be a moment of laughter when something goes wrong or the peace of watching your partner sleep. These little moments of happiness are just as important as they are grounding.

Navigating the twin tides of joy and anxiety as you prepare to welcome a new life into the world is no small feat. But you can balance these emotions effectively with a bit of mindfulness, a positive outlook, and a focus on the small moments. Doing so will make the journey more enjoyable and deepen your connection to the experience, allowing you to be fully present for the highs, the lows, and everything in between. It's not about getting rid of the anxiety or increasing the joy; it's about giving space for both, embracing them, and moving forward with confidence. And before you know it, you'll be more than just a spectator in your own circus—you'll be the ringmaster, guiding your family through the wonderful spectacle of life.

CHAPTER 2
HORMONE HARMONY:
EMOTIONAL SUPPORT STRATEGIES

Ever feel like you're trying to understand an alien language without a translator or a guidebook? That's what it's like trying to figure out pregnancy hormones, but you're not alone. The key is empathy, and that's what we're going to talk about in this chapter. Think of yourself as an emotional archaeologist, digging through the layers of mood swings and emotional changes until you find the buried treasure of understanding and connection.

2.1 MASTERING THE ART OF PREGNANCY EMPATHY

Recognizing Emotional Changes

So, your partner is all over the place emotionally, thanks to being pregnant. One moment, she's laughing at a cat video; the next, she's crying at a commercial about a happy family. It might be confusing, but these emotional swings are about as normal as wanting pickles in the middle of the night. Pregnancy isn't just a physical journey; it's an emotional one, too, thanks to hormonal changes that can make your calm and collected partner feel like she's in the middle of an emotional tornado.

Understanding these changes is your first step. It's like realizing that the rollercoaster isn't malfunctioning; it's designed to be this wild. Hormones, particularly estrogen and progesterone, can intensify your partner's emotions. It doesn't mean she's permanently changed; she's just more sensitive now. Knowing that can help you get through this without taking everything personally or being confused by her new normal.

Active Listening Skills

Honing your active listening skills isn't about nodding while you mentally compile your to-do list. Active listening involves fully engaging with what your partner is expressing. When she shares how she's feeling, give her your undivided attention. Turn off the TV, put down your phone, and actually listen. That means hearing her words, noticing her tone, watching her body language, and letting her know you understand through verbal and non-verbal communication. "It sounds like you're struggling with this" can go a long way, as opposed to, "I don't see why this is such a big deal."

Empathetic Engagement

Engaging with empathy means connecting with the emotions behind your partner's words. It's about validating her feelings without immediately rushing to solve problems. For instance, if she's feeling insecure about her body changes, instead of saying, "You still look great to me," try, "It sounds like you're struggling with these changes. It's got to be tough, but I'm here for you." This kind of response acknowledges her feelings without dismissing them. It reinforces that you're her partner in this journey, not just a bystander.

Cultivating Patience and Understanding

Patience is the key during pregnancy. There will be times when your partner gets snippy over something trivial or when she needs the same reassurances over and over again. This is where patience comes in. You have to remember that these mood swings are not a reflection of the strength of your relationship; they are just part of the ups and downs of pregnancy.

It all starts with understanding. Try to put yourself in her shoes. Pregnancy can feel like being constantly judged by a panel of harsh critics (thank you, hormones!), and what she needs most is your unconditional support. When things get tough, take a deep breath, give her the benefit of the doubt, and remember that this phase isn't forever. It is like building a bridge over troubled waters if you can remain calm and supportive, even when you don't fully understand what she is going through. It is an investment in your relationship, ensuring it will still stand when the hormones calm down.

2.2 EFFECTIVE COMMUNICATION DURING HORMONAL SHIFTS

Navigating the hormonal rapids during pregnancy can sometimes feel like trying to have a deep conversation while riding a rollercoaster—it's thrilling, unpredictable, and you're not always sure you're heard over the din. Understanding how hormonal fluctuations can profoundly impact your partner's mood and emotions is akin to being handed a map in this amusement park; it doesn't stop the ride, but it sure helps you know what to expect around the next bend.

During pregnancy, the body is a cocktail shaker of hormones, each adding flavor to your partner's emotional state. These hormonal changes can sometimes transform your usually cool partner into a hot mess of feelings, not because they want to keep you on your toes. Hormones like estrogen and progesterone are doing the heavy lifting in preparing her body to carry and nourish your baby, and a side effect is that they can also amplify emotions or trigger sudden mood swings. Recognizing these shifts as hormonal influences can help you maintain perspective, reminding you that these moments are not personal critiques but passing storms.

Communication in these times is like threading a needle while wearing boxing gloves; it requires precision and patience, but it's not impossible. Keeping the lines of communication open means ensuring that you're both heard and understood, no matter the emotional climate. This can be as simple as establishing regular check-ins where you both share your feelings and thoughts. Think of it as a daily debrief, where the goal isn't to fix problems but to share experiences. When stress or emotions run high, adapt your communication style. Sometimes, this might mean focusing more on listening rather than offering solutions, or it might involve using affirmations that acknowledge her feelings before jumping into problem-solving mode.

Navigating disagreements when hormones play the puppeteer can add an extra layer of complexity. Here, the key is sensitivity—recognizing that your partner might react more intensely than usual and that these reactions are often temporary. Approach disagreements with a strategy that emphasizes de-escalation; take a breath before responding, use "I" statements that focus on your feelings rather than accusatory "you" statements, and propose pausing contentious issues until you can both approach them with cooler heads. For example, instead of saying, "You never listen to me," try saying, "I feel unheard when my thoughts aren't considered." It's about picking battles wisely and recognizing when to give space and when to engage.

Creating a supportive environment is about building a physically and emotionally nurturing nest. This goes beyond fluffy pillows and comfy furniture; it's about fostering an atmosphere where open, honest communication is the norm. Encourage an environment where it's safe to express vulnerabilities without fear of judgment. Leaving notes of appreciation or scheduling a surprise date night are small gestures that can help maintain a positive atmosphere at home. It's about making your living space a sanctuary where stress is managed and emotions are respected.

Remember, effective communication during hormonal shifts isn't just about navigating the high seas of mood swings; it's about ensuring that the lines of communication remain open and strong, providing a lifeline that keeps you both connected through every twist and turn. These strategies fortify your relationship, ensuring that you emerge from the pregnancy journey stronger and more in tune with each other than ever.

Transitioning into the next chapter, we'll explore how all these emotional and communication strategies play out in the real world, offering practical tips to help you apply what you've learned. Get ready to take these insights from theory to practice, ensuring you're surviving and thriving together in this incredible phase of your lives.

CHAPTER 3
BUMP AND RUN:
THE FIRST TRIMESTER

Imagine you've just been given the keys to a complex and somewhat mysterious spaceship, and your job, should you choose to accept it, is to fly this thing smoothly through the first critical stage of its flight. Welcome to the first trimester, new dad. This isn't just any flight. This is a three-month voyage where the stakes are as high as your stress levels are about to be. But don't worry because I'm here to help you through these initial weeks when the magic begins but isn't quite visible.

3.1 WEEKS 1-3: READY, SET, GROW

Welcome to the wild ride of conception! It's more than just a romantic evening and hopeful intentions; it's a full-on biological Grand Prix. Imagine millions of eager participants (sperm) dashing toward a single, incredibly well-guarded prize: the egg. Only the fastest, most resilient swimmer gets the honor of fertilization. This monumental meeting starts the incredible process of creating a new life, leading to the formation of a zygote. Think of it as the first leg of an epic relay race, where the baton passes at lightning speed.

Week 1-3		
Precious Progress	**Maternal Marvels**	**Father's Finesse**
Millions of sperm compete to fertilize the egg, starting the baby's development—think "Survivor: Conception Island."	Hormone levels increase, secretly preparing her body before she even knows she's pregnant.	Encourage healthy eating—fruits, veggies, lean proteins. Think of food as fuel, like stocking a marathon runner's fridge.
Rapid cell division begins, shaping your baby's future traits, like constructing a complex LEGO model piece by piece.	Hormones ready the uterine lining for implantation.	Engage in stress-reducing activities like prenatal yoga or binge-watching shows. It's about nurturing a thriving environment.

As you navigate these first few weeks of pregnancy, remember that even though much of what's happening is invisible to the naked eye, your role as a supportive partner is clear as day. Your efforts to champion a healthy lifestyle, reduce stress, and make small sacrifices do not go unnoticed. This early phase is about setting the stage for what's to come, preparing for the incredible transformation. So, buckle up, Dad-to-Be, and get ready for the ride of a lifetime. Welcome to fatherhood; it will be one heck of an adventure filled with humor, love, and plenty of dad jokes.

3.2 WEEK 4: SEEING DOUBLE...LINES

So you're staring down at a pregnancy test, and there it is—not one, but two pink lines. Congratulations, it's official! You're about to be a dad. This moment, charged with excitement and a healthy dose of "what now?" is more than a positive test result. It's the green light at the starting line of a thrilling and transformative ride.

This is the foundation of your journey—not just as expectant parents but as a team ready to tackle the incredible adventure of parenthood. Embrace this early stage with all its subtle signs and significant implications, laying the groundwork for a supportive, informed, and loving partnership. Your role now is crucial, and every step you take together strengthens the bond and prepares you both for the remarkable journey ahead.

30 FIRST-TIME FATHER FUNDAMENTALS:

Week 4		
Precious Progress	**Maternal Marvels**	**Father's Finesse**
The blastocyst, a tiny ball of cells that will develop into the placenta and baby, implants in the womb, securing a nutrient-rich spot.	Early signs like mild cramping and spotting mark the start of pregnancy. They are subtle but significant.	Start planning prenatal care, discussing support needs, and choosing the right healthcare provider, like plotting a journey on a map.
The amniotic sac starts to form around the blastocyst, providing a protective environment for the developing embryo.	One of the earliest signs of pregnancy is a missed menstrual period, which often prompts women to take a pregnancy test.	Be understanding and patient with mood swings and emotional fluctuations. Listening and providing reassurance can go a long way.

3.3 WEEK 5: TINY TENANT

Welcome to week five, where things start getting real, both in terms of what's happening inside and how it's starting to hit home that you're going to be a dad. The embryo, your future son or daughter, is now beginning to take on a shape that resembles a tadpole if you squint a bit and use your imagination. This might not sound like the cuddly infant you're dreaming of, but it's a crucial stage in development. What's genuinely awe-inspiring is that this is the week when the heart begins to form. Yes, that's right—the heart. It's just a simple tube, but it's already starting to beat, pumping blood through that tiny body. This isn't just any heartbeat; it's the rhythm of a new life you helped create. It's a profound moment that brings the gravity of fatherhood into sharp, thrilling focus. Picture a heart the size of a poppy seed, already working hard. If that's not a miracle, what is?

Week 5		
Precious Progress	**Maternal Marvels**	**Father's Finesse**
The embryo's heart begins to form and beat, pumping blood.	Morning sickness can strike anytime, turning favorite foods into foes.	Attend prenatal visits to hear the heartbeat and demonstrate long-term support.
Foundations for major organs are laid, setting the stage for future development like a winning team strategy.	Hormonal changes cause breast tenderness, making gentle hugs feel like navigating minefields.	Take over chores, handle meals, ensure hydration, and keep easy snacks available to ease her nausea.
The neural tube, which will become the baby's brain, spinal cord, and backbone, begins to develop.	Profound exhaustion makes daily activities feel like a marathon.	Listen, comfort, and validate her feelings, recognizing the early challenges and triumphs of creating life.

This week is a mix of wonder and challenge, of awe at the rapid developments happening in such a tiny form, and empathy for the physical toll it's taking on your partner. It's a time to marvel at life's miracles and rise to the occasion as a supportive partner. The reality of fatherhood is setting in, bringing a profound sense of connection to the little life you're helping to create and the person you're embarking on this incredible adventure with.

3.4 WEEK 6: FEEL THE RHYTHM

Step into week six, where the real magic of pregnancy starts to get up close and personal. If you thought the past weeks were a whirlwind, hold onto your hat because now, you're entering what could be the main event of the first trimester: the heartbeat. This isn't just any old thump-thump; it's your baby's heartbeat, and it's about to play the sweetest music you've ever heard. Until now, your little one has been busy behind the scenes, but with the commencement of this vital pulse, development shifts into high gear. Major organs are taking shape, and that tiny heart, now beating robustly, ensures that nutrients and oxygen are delivered to help each organ develop properly.

Week 6		
Precious Progress	**Maternal Marvels**	**Father's Finesse**
Your baby is about the size of a lentil, measuring around 1/8 to 1/4 inch (about 4-6 mm) in length.	As the baby develops, your partner may experience intense morning sickness, making even favorite foods unbearable.	To help manage morning sickness, offer bland, easy-to-digest foods and ensure frequent, small meals. Hydration is crucial.
Like an orchestra tuning up, major organs such as the liver, kidneys, and lungs begin forming, fueled by the heartbeat.	Hormonal fluctuations can turn minor annoyances into major ordeals and intensify emotional responses.	Small gestures like back rubs, foot massages, or simply sitting quietly together can provide significant relief. Encourage open, non-judgmental communication about her feelings.

This week is about more than just surviving; it's about nurturing—the baby and your relationship. As you both listen to that little heartbeat, let it remind you of the rhythm of the life you're building together. It's a delicate dance of give and take, support and independence, and always love. So keep your ears, arms, and heart open. The music is just beginning; you don't want to miss a single note.

3.5 WEEK 7: FROM BLOB TO BABE

Week 7		
Precious Progress	**Maternal Marvels**	**Father's Finesse**
The baby is about the size of a blueberry, measuring approximately 1/3 inch (about 8-10 mm) in length.	Her sense of smell intensifies, making previously pleasant aromas overwhelming and potentially unpleasant.	Reduce strong scents at home; opt for natural or fragrance-free options and ensure good ventilation.
Neurons multiply rapidly, up to 100,000 per minute, laying the foundation for future abilities and preferences.	This sensory enhancement helps steer her away from harmful substances, a natural safeguard for the baby.	Adapt to her changing food preferences to ensure she receives necessary nutrients, managing food aversions sensitively.

Welcome to week seven, where your little one is making strides from a generic blob to something resembling a babe. It's like watching a sculptor at work, starting with a rough outline and gradually defining the masterpiece. This week, that masterpiece is your baby's face and brain. Yes, facial features are beginning to form. Tiny indentations that will soon blossom into eyes and ears and the faint outline of what will become the nose and mouth are emerging. It's like the universe's most precious dot-to-dot, where each connection sparks new potential.

As week seven unfolds, with each new facial feature and every brain cell that forms, you're getting closer to meeting your little bundle of joy. And while your baby's features become more defined, your role as a supportive partner does, too. It's about more than just riding out the changes; it's about actively enhancing the journey for your partner and the little one on the way. Embrace the changes, prepare for the adjustments, and remember each step you take now is a building block for your family's future.

3.6 WEEK 8: LIMBS IN THE LIMELIGHT

Week 8		
Precious Progress	**Maternal Marvels**	**Father's Finesse**
The baby is about the size of a raspberry, measuring around 1/2 inch to 3/4 inch (12-20 mm) in length and weighing approximately 1 gram.	Her body supports the baby by increasing blood volume to 50%, enhancing nutrient and oxygen delivery.	The first ultrasound is a significant event; think of it as the premiere of your baby's debut.
Early muscle development initiates movement, like a mini athlete's gentle warm-up.	The increased blood volume can cause dizziness as her body adjusts.	Prepare necessary documents and questions about the baby's development and expected symptoms, showing your full engagement.

Roll out the red carpet because week eight brings a premiere-worthy development: the formation of your baby's fingers, toes, and first movements. Up to this point, your little one's limbs have been more like tiny buds, but now they're stretching out, getting ready to wave hello. Those fingers and toes are sprouting, not yet ready to grasp or wiggle purposefully, but marking a pivotal shift in your baby's journey from a mere cluster of cells to a more recognizable human form. It's like seeing an architect meticulously draft each line, constructing a detailed blueprint for a grand structure.

Encourage your partner to drink plenty of water for her health and clearer ultrasound images.

As you prepare to see your baby for the first time, remember that this ultrasound is more than just a check-up. It's a window into the womb, offering you both a glimpse of the life you're shaping together. It's a moment to celebrate, to marvel at, and to reflect on the journey you're both on. So take a deep breath, hold her hand, and step into this experience with as much love and enthusiasm as you can muster. The road ahead is as exciting as it is sacred, and every step, every heartbeat, and every little kick is a part of the incredible narrative of your growing family.

3.7 WEEK 9: PEEK-A-BOO! I SEE YOU

As you enter week nine, gear up for one of the most exhilarating experiences—the first ultrasound. This isn't just a routine check-up; it's the grand premiere, where you can see your baby's debut on the small screen. It's like the curtain finally lifting on a show you've been waiting to see for what feels like forever. Only, in this show, the star is your soon-to-be little one, and the co-stars are the awe and joy lighting up your faces. This ultrasound marks a profound moment in confirming the pregnancy and making it all the more real. You're not just expecting; you're visually connected now to the tiny human you and your partner are creating.

Week 9		
Precious Progress	**Maternal Marvels**	**Father's Finesse**
The baby is roughly the size of a green olive, measuring 0.9 (2.3 cm) inches long and weighing 2 grams.	Leukorrhea, the milky discharge, protects the birth canal from infections, acting as a natural barrier against bacteria.	Engage actively during the ultrasound. This scan checks the baby's health and due date. Ask questions and show interest, enhancing this significant experience for both of you.
The eyes are developing more fully, with the retinas forming and the lenses taking shape.	Hormonal changes can slow down digestion, leading to bloating and gas.	Encourage your partner to eat smaller, more frequent meals and avoid foods that cause gas. Walking is a gentle exercise that can also help with digestion.

For me, seeing that first ultrasound was a rollercoaster of emotions—mainly excitement mixed with a bit of terror. "Please don't be twins, please don't be twins," was my silent prayer as we walked into the appointment. The technician pointed to the screen, and there it was—a tiny flickering heartbeat. Honestly, if she hadn't pointed it out, I'd still be staring at that grainy black-and-white image like some abstract art. (Pro tip: have the technician circle and draw arrows on the printout for clarity.) When she confirmed there was just one baby in there, I breathed an audible sigh of relief. "That's our kid—singular, thank goodness." My relief was so apparent that even the technician chuckled.

As you watch the life you've created together, take shape on that screen, let the reality sink in. This ultrasound isn't just a medical procedure; it's a window into the new life you're crafting together. It's a peek into the future, a glimpse of the adventures, and a profound reminder of the life-changing role you're about to step into. So take it all in, cherish your baby's first images, and let the love and excitement fill you up. This is just the beginning, and what a beautiful beginning it is.

3.8 WEEK 10: LEVELING UP IN THE WOMB

Week 10		
Precious Progress	**Maternal Marvels**	**Father's Finesse**
The transition from embryo to fetus indicates decreased miscarriage risk and the start of specialized growth.	The reduced risk of miscarriage brings emotional relief, like clear skies following a storm, renewing spirit and hope.	Ensure a diet rich in essential nutrients to support the fetus's rapid growth—like fueling for a marathon.
Basic structures form; organs start functioning. The fetus is now a bustling miniature construction site.	This energy may bring back some normalcy and pre-pregnancy activities, highlighting the uniqueness of each pregnancy journey.	Engage and respond to her emotional changes; discuss plans to strengthen connection and provide excitement.

Mark your calendars because week ten is a big one in the tiny world of your developing baby. If there were ever a time to say things are getting serious, it's now. This week, the little life inside that special person is making a grand transition from being an embryo to officially being called a fetus. It's not just a change in terminology; it's a significant milestone that signals a crucial decrease in the risk of miscarriage and the start of more intense growth phases. Think of it as graduating from a tricycle to a bicycle—things are about to speed up!

As you both navigate this critical week, remember the transition to fetal status is more than just a developmental milestone; it's a profound reminder of the life you are both nurturing. Every meal shared, every discussion about the future, and every step taken to prepare for upcoming tests are threads in the fabric of your growing family. Keep weaving with care, love, and an eye toward the future you are both creating. This journey is just beginning, and each step forward brings you closer to meeting your little one. Enjoy the ride!

3.9 WEEK 11: HERE COMES THE BUMP

Now that you've cruised past the first ten weeks, brace yourself for the visible changes that make pregnancy undeniably real to everyone, not just the two of you who are in on the secret. Welcome to week 11, where the baby bump starts making its grand entrance. This isn't just any bump; it's the first tangible proof of the new life brewing inside. It's small, sure, but it's enough to turn your partner's morning routine into a quest for comfy pants.

Up till now, the baby's been tucked away, growing quietly. But as you hit week 11, the uterus begins to expand above the pelvis, and voila, you start seeing the physical manifestation of the pregnancy. It's a bit like watching the first shoots of a plant sprout from the soil, a tiny yet exhilarating hint of the growth beneath. This bump might be slight, easily hidden under a loose shirt, but its psychological impact can be significant. It's a beacon of the changes yet to come, a symbol that there's no turning back now. The pregnancy becomes something you can see and touch, not just talk about.

	Week 11	
Precious Progress	**Maternal Marvels**	**Father's Finesse**
As your baby's body structures intensely differentiate, genitalia form but are too early to identify by ultrasound.	The emerging baby bump may stir a mix of pride and anxiety, impacting body image and emotional well-being.	Turn maternity wear shopping into a fun, uplifting date to boost her confidence as her body changes.
The baby's brain rapidly expands within a disproportionately large head, laying early foundations for post-birth learning.	Hormonal changes might lead to a "pregnancy glow" or, for some, skin issues like acne.	Encourage her to maintain her personal style with maternity wear that reflects her tastes, enhancing her journey into motherhood.

As you wrap up week 11, the pregnancy becomes more visible and tangible. It's a week of growth, change, and preparation. It's about embracing the new curves, celebrating the tiny developments, and supporting each other through every little change. So, as the bump grows, let your partnership grow stronger, too. This is a beautiful phase, a visible reminder of the life you will welcome into the world together. Enjoy, cherish, and, as always, keep stepping forward with love and laughter.

3.10 WEEK 12: FUELING THE BUMP

As you hit the twelfth week of this adventure, you're not just closing the chapter on the first trimester; you're stepping into a pivotal arena where the placenta, a remarkable organ unique to pregnancy, takes center stage. This isn't just any organ—it's a temporary but powerhouse addition that your partner's body crafts specifically for this gig. The placenta is the ultimate multitasker: part nutrient superhighway, part waste management system, and part hormone factory. It's all about keeping the baby nourished, clean, and growing in a perfectly balanced hormonal environment.

Week 12		
Precious Progress	**Maternal Marvels**	**Father's Finesse**
The placenta, connected via the umbilical cord, supplies nutrients and oxygen to your baby and removes waste.	As the placenta ramps up hormone production, your partner may experience less morning sickness.	Celebrate the end of the first trimester, acknowledging the significant hurdles you've overcome together.
The placenta produces essential hormones like progesterone and human placental lactogen, acting as a built-in pharmacy for pregnancy health.	Reduced nausea might lead to increased energy, allowing her to enjoy daily activities and stabilize her routine.	Mark this milestone with a special meal or quiet celebration to reflect on your journey and future.

As you close the chapter on the first trimester, take a moment to appreciate how far you've come and how much growth lies ahead. It's a journey unlike any other, and every step, every challenge, and every victory is a part of the incredible story you are writing together. So, celebrate this milestone, enjoy the decrease in morning sickness, and prepare for the exciting developments in the second trimester.

CHAPTER 4
BANKROLLING BABY:
PENNIES, PACIFIERS, AND PLANS

Our first try at budgeting for the baby was a total disaster. We wanted to do the right thing, so we got a computer and started figuring out our finances. But we didn't know the first thing about how to do that. We started with the essentials—crib, stroller, diapers—and then began to get ridiculous. My wife insisted we needed a baby food processor. I argued we should get a baby monitor with night vision and a walkie-talkie feature (because our baby would obviously need to talk to us covertly).

Then we realized we'd forgotten about the hospital bills and prenatal vitamins. We scrambled to fix it, adding rows to the spreadsheet and changing numbers around like we were playing financial Jenga.

Our biggest mistake was not realizing how many diapers a baby goes through daily. We had planned for about 100 diapers a month. But by the end of the first month, we were overwhelmed with dirty diapers and found ourselves making late-night runs to the store.

Looking back, we can laugh, but one thing we learned is that budgeting for a baby isn't about getting it right; it's about adapting as you go.

Hopefully, this chapter will guide you through creating a realistic budget, understanding the essential costs, and finding intelligent ways to save without sacrificing quality. Whether you're a financial wizard or a complete novice, these insights will help you confidently navigate the financial side of first-time fatherhood.

4.1 BUDGETING FOR BABY: A REALISTIC GUIDE

Initial Costs

Diving headfirst into fatherhood means dealing with some upfront expenses that can make even the most financially responsible of us do a double-take. You've got everything from hospital bills—which can feel like you're being charged for a week-long vacation—to setting up a nursery, which probably looks more like a storage room than a place fit for an infant. Here's the breakdown: hospital stays can vary, but remember, it's more than just a room. It's the doctors, the nurses, the medications, and that magical moment when you hear the first cry—none of which comes cheap. Then there's the nursery; you need a crib, a firm mattress, a changing table, and a decorating scheme that doesn't make you want to gag.

Creating a Baby Budget

Now, before you freak out over costs, let's talk strategy. Making a baby budget isn't just a good idea; it's your new favorite pastime. Start with a simple spreadsheet or a baby budgeting app (yes, there are apps for that). Add in your usual expenses, then start adding in baby-related items. Be thorough. Diapers, wipes, baby gear, and a line item that just says 'miscellaneous' because, trust me, unexpected costs pop up like midnight cravings for pickles and ice cream.

What's Really Essential?

This is where you get to be a CEO. Not all baby expenses are the same. Prioritize! Yes, you need a baby monitor, but does it need HD video streaming capabilities, or will a basic audio one be sufficient? Diapers are non-negotiable, but you may decide that designer baby outfits with matching hats might not be essential. Focus on what is essential for safety and daily care and what is just nice to have. This is not about being cheap; it's about being smart and making sure you spend your money where it counts.

Week 11		
Precious Progress	**Maternal Marvels**	**Father's Finesse**
As your baby's body structures intensely differentiate, genitalia form but are too early to identify by ultrasound.	The emerging baby bump may stir a mix of pride and anxiety, impacting body image and emotional well-being.	Turn maternity wear shopping into a fun, uplifting date to boost her confidence as her body changes.
The baby's brain rapidly expands within a disproportionately large head, laying early foundations for post-birth learning.	Hormonal changes might lead to a "pregnancy glow" or, for some, skin issues like acne.	Encourage her to maintain her personal style with maternity wear that reflects her tastes, enhancing her journey into motherhood.

Harnessing Tech to Tame the Budget Beast

Remember when I mentioned apps? This is where they come in handy. Financial tools and apps can track your spending, remind you of bill due dates, and suggest where to cut costs. Some apps are designed specifically for new parents, offering features like savings trackers for college funds or reminders for upcoming pediatrician visits. Think of these tools as your financial sidekicks, here to make money management more manageable.

Navigating the financial aspects of new parenthood can be as challenging as assembling a thousand-piece puzzle without a picture. But with a firm grasp on initial costs, a reasonable budgeting plan, and the right financial tools, you'll easily handle this aspect of fatherhood. And remember, you don't just want to get by financially; you want to thrive, ensuring that you and your family are safe, prepared, and ready for all the fun (and chaos) a baby can bring. So, let's keep this financial advice going as we look into insurance and healthcare in the next section, making sure you're as ready as possible for the arrival of your little one.

4.2 INSURANCE AND HEALTHCARE: NAVIGATING THE MAZE

Navigating insurance and healthcare for pregnancy might seem more complicated than explaining why you need five different types of screwdrivers to someone who's never used a tool in their life. But like those screwdrivers, each part of your insurance policy has a different purpose. First, you need to understand your health insurance coverage. Think of your insurance policy as a manual for your car; it's not the most exciting thing to read, but when a warning light goes off, or in this case, when you're having a baby, you'll be glad you know what's in it. This will tell you what's covered, from prenatal check-ups to postnatal care. You need to understand terms like co-pays (a fixed amount for a specific medical service), deductibles (the amount you pay before the insurance takes over), and out-of-pocket maximums (the most you will have to pay for covered services in a single year) because, let's face it, babies are expensive even before they're born.

Now that you know what to look for, it's time to ask your insurance provider some key questions. This isn't just a friendly conversation; it's more like a scene from a detective show where the detective tries to get every last detail. Ask about the specifics of maternity and newborn care coverage. How many ultrasounds are covered? What if there is an emergency during delivery? Are there any preferred hospitals or doctors you should know about? Knowing these details can save you a lot of grief and money. You want to be able to focus on your partner and new baby when the time comes, not calling insurance from the hospital.

Next, let's discuss ensuring your partner and baby have the necessary healthcare. Think of yourself as the general manager of a top-tier sports team, and you wouldn't send your players out without the right gear, medical staff, and a game plan, right? For your partner, prenatal check-ups are non-negotiable. These appointments ensure she and the baby are healthy and can catch any potential issues early. For your newborn, selecting a pediatrician is a critical play. This doctor will be your go-to for everything from vaccination schedules to middle-of-the-night fevers, so choose someone you both trust and feel comfortable with. Set up an initial meeting to discuss everything from breastfeeding support to who to call when the baby's first cold strikes.

Finally, let's talk about unexpected medical costs. Even with all the planning, life can throw you a curveball. Having some money set aside for unexpected healthcare costs can be a lifesaver. It's not about having a certain amount of money set aside, but enough that you can handle any surprises without putting your family in financial jeopardy. Whether it's extra tests during pregnancy or unexpected procedures during delivery, having a plan to manage these costs can keep you focused on what's important.

4.3 SAVING FOR THE FUTURE: EDUCATION AND EMERGENCY FUNDS

When it comes to fatherhood, you're not just managing diaper duties and midnight lullabies; you're also stepping up as the CFO of your newly expanded family. This role involves some forward-thinking, specifically around squirreling away funds for future needs like education and those unexpected curveballs life loves to throw. Let's start with the education fund. While it may seem early to start saving for college when your child has yet to be introduced to the world, college tuition rates have steadily increased. If you don't start saving now, you might be unable to afford it when the time comes.

One of your best bets for an education fund is a 529 plan. This isn't just any savings account; it's a state-sponsored plan with tantalizing tax advantages. Think of it as a tax-free growth booster for your child's college cash. The money you put in grows tax-free and can be withdrawn tax-free if you use it for qualified educational expenses. This could range from tuition fees to books and even room and board under certain conditions. Different states offer different flavors of 529 plans, each with its own perks, so picking one can feel like choosing the right ice cream flavor—it's worth taking some time to get it right.

But life isn't just about preparing for college; it's also about handling the unexpected without breaking into a cold sweat. That's where your emergency fund comes in. Think of this as your financial fire extinguisher—it's there to tackle small fires before they become infernos. Whether it's a sudden job loss, a car breakdown, or an unexpected home repair, having an emergency fund means you're ready. How much to stash? A good rule of thumb is three to six months' worth of living expenses. Yes, it sounds like a lot, but starting small can still give you a cushion. Even if it's just a little each month, it's about building a habit, a safety net that grows over time.

Now, let's talk about some practical ways to save money. Babies are expensive, and it's not like they come with a money-back guarantee. First, consider your needs over your wants. This doesn't mean skimping on essentials, but it does mean not buying that overpriced baby outfit they'll grow out of in a week. Next, get friendly with local parents' groups—they often organize swap meets where you can trade baby gear and clothes with other parents, keeping your costs down and recycling items with plenty of life left in them. And let's not forget about sales and discounts—sign up for newsletters and alerts from your favorite baby stores, and don't be shy about using coupons. These small savings can add up, giving you more wiggle room in your budget to allocate funds toward saving for the big stuff, like education and emergencies.

4.4 COST-SAVING TIPS FOR EXPECTANT FATHERS

Navigating the financial waters of fatherhood doesn't mean you have to drain the bank. Let's roll up our sleeves and dig into some wallet-friendly strategies that keep the cash flow more "ka-ching" than "ka-chunk." Starting with the age-old wisdom of second-hand and hand-me-downs—this is your new best friend in the realm of baby gear. Think about it. How much use does a newborn really get out of that designer onesie before it's more food splatter than fabric? Tapping into the world of gently used baby items can save you a small fortune, and here's the kicker—it's not just about saving money but also about sustainability.

Baby gear, especially big-ticket items like cribs, strollers, and high chairs, are often used for only a short time in the grand scheme of things. This makes second-hand stores, online marketplaces, and even your cousin's attic great places to find good, barely used items. But here's a tip: always check for safety recalls and expiration dates on items like car seats and cribs. Safety is the one area where you don't want to skimp. When you find safe, second-hand gear, you're saving money and doing your part to be eco-friendly by giving these items a second life. And let's be honest: teaching your child about sustainability from day one is a win-win.

Moving on to do-it-yourself projects. Welcome to your new weekend activity. Whether it's refinishing an old dresser into a changing table with nothing but some sandpaper and a dream or making your own mobiles that don't cost more than your first car, DIY is the way to go if you want to save money and add a personal touch to your baby's space. YouTube and Pinterest will be your new best friends in the world of DIY baby gear. You can knit your own little hats and even build your own crib. The possibilities are endless. DIY is not only a money-saver but a story you can tell. Imagine your child growing up and learning that their favorite bookshelf was made by you, filled with love, hope, and probably a little sweat. These personal touches make a room more than just a room.

Let's talk about smart shopping for necessities you can't make yourself or find used. Sales are your best bet here. Subscribing to baby store newsletters may seem small, but it gets you in line for deals and exclusive offers. Buying in bulk can also save you a lot, especially for things like diapers and wipes. Consider also looking into subscription services that deliver at regular intervals for a discounted rate. Just remember to buy strategically, not excessively. If you time your purchases with sales like Black Friday or end-of-season clearances, you can save much more than you might think.

Let's not forget the financial resources and assistance programs available to new parents. Many governments and organizations offer programs that can help with healthcare costs, food, and even childcare. This could include things like tax credits for dependent care or help with medical bills. It may take some research, but the savings could be worth it. Local parenting groups and online forums can also be great resources, offering advice on everything from the best budget-friendly baby products to how to work with government assistance programs. It's about building a network of resources to help you emotionally and financially.

Adopting these strategies saves you money now and sets the stage for sensible, responsible spending that will benefit your family for years. Whether that means shopping smart, doing things yourself, or taking advantage of local resources, the point is to welcome your new baby without worrying about money. By making these sound financial decisions now, you set yourself up to concentrate on what's important in the future—raising your child in a loving, joyful, and financially secure environment.

CHAPTER 5
GROWING AND GLOWING:
THE 2ND TRIMESTER

If the first trimester was a sneak preview, consider the second trimester the feature film in which your baby stars in "Growth Spurts Galore: The Uterine Chronicles." Welcome, Dad-to-Be, to the golden era of pregnancy, where the plot thickens, the belly pops, and your partner might start feeling like herself again, minus the tiny human doing somersaults inside her.

5.1 WEEK 13: BABY'S BIGGER, BETTER SEQUEL

Welcome to Week 13 of the Pregnancy Playbook—your guide to the "second trimester," where the fun continues! As we roll out the red carpet into this blockbuster phase, imagine it as the bigger, better sequel to the somewhat nail-biting origin story you've been dealing with. Like any good sequel, this one promises more excitement, less nausea, and even, dare we say, a splash of glamor (or as glamorous as she can feel with a growing belly).

Week 13		
Precious Progress	**Maternal Marvels**	**Father's Finesse**
Your baby starts tuning their vocal cords, preparing for future cries and laughs.	Post-morning sickness phase, your partner may feel energized and ready for prenatal activities and nursery planning.	Encourage a balance of activity and rest to avoid burnout during this energized phase.
Your baby also begins practicing swallowing, an essential step for developing their digestive system.	The growing uterus puts increased pressure on the bladder, leading to more frequent trips to the bathroom.	Join in the nursery setup, support every baby development milestone, and maintain positivity.

As you both navigate this exciting middle stretch, remember that the second trimester is like the sweet spot of pregnancy—enough energy to feel human again and enough happening inside the womb to keep the anticipation high. Enjoy this phase, keep the humor up, and here's to making memories one baby kick and paint swatch at a time!

5.2 WEEK 14: MILE-A-MINUTE CHANGES

Strap in, folks! We've hit Week 14, where your baby transforms from a tiny blip on the ultrasound into a full-blown manufacturing powerhouse. Think of your growing little one as a factory during wartime production—gears grinding, assembly lines flowing, and products (i.e., tiny human parts) rolling out non-stop. Welcome to the sprint in development that leaves even the most ambitious city planners in awe.

Week 14		
Precious Progress	**Maternal Marvels**	**Father's Finesse**
The liver and spleen are busy manufacturing blood cells crucial for transporting oxygen and fighting infections.	Your partner's appetite surges, fueling the body's intensive building efforts.	Prepare meals rich in iron and protein to support your baby's growth.
Your baby's unique fingerprints are forming.	Her body shifts from survival to thrive mode, turning every meal into building blocks for the baby.	Adapt meals to manage her cravings and aversions, ensuring nutrition remains appealing and fun.

As you both navigate through the mile-a-minute changes of Week 14, remember, this isn't just a journey through pregnancy—it's the build-up to the grand unveiling of your newest family member. With each passing day, you're ensuring the tiny factory inside her runs smoothly and cementing the teamwork that makes this whole parenting adventure worthwhile. So keep those nutrients coming, embrace the transformations, and maybe, just maybe, start thinking of baby names that mean "mighty" or "builder"—because, at this rate, you'll have a little powerhouse on your hands!

5.3 WEEK 15: KICKOFF TIME

Welcome to Week 15, where your baby's starting to give their best audition for a future in rhythmic gymnastics—inside the womb! This week, the dance routines get a bit more complex with the debut of the baby's first subtle movements, known as "quickening." It's like the first rehearsal for a lifetime of moves and grooves. Let's not just focus on those internal dance moves; a lot is happening on the main stage (a.k.a. mommy's body) that deserves a spotlight, too!

Week 15		
Precious Progress	**Maternal Marvels**	**Father's Finesse**
The baby's skeleton continues to harden from soft cartilage into bone. The joints and limbs are becoming more functional, and the baby is practicing movements by kicking and flexing.	As the uterus expands, the ligaments supporting it stretch, which can cause sharp, brief pain on one or both sides of the lower abdomen.	Stay sensitive to her shifting emotions, sharing joy, and offering support.
Taste buds and sensory systems are forming, tuning up for life's full symphony outside the womb.	Increased blood flow to mucous membranes can cause nasal congestion or even nosebleeds.	Support her engagement in gentle exercise to enhance energy, circulation, and overall well-being.

As you waltz through Week 15, enjoy every flutter and kick as signs of your baby's growth and vitality. This week is about syncing with the rhythms of pregnancy, both the seen and the unseen. Keep the dialogue open, stay attuned to her needs, and continue crafting that perfect environment of support and love as you both prepare for the crescendo of childbirth. Here's to more kicks, growth, and shared moments in this amazing journey!

5.4 WEEK 16: SENSORY OVERLOAD

Welcome to Week 16, also known as the "Great Sensory Tune-up!" This week, we're not just growing; we're getting an auditory overhaul, with your baby's tiny ears gearing up to catch the latest gossip, the daily dose of dog barks, or that playlist you've been overplaying. Oh, and let's not forget those nifty new moves your partner might notice as your baby practices for their future Olympic gymnastics career.

Week 16		
Precious Progress	**Maternal Marvels**	**Father's Finesse**
Your baby can hear external sounds, tuning into their first soundscape.	The baby's movements intensify the pregnancy experience, offering joy and reassurance of healthy development.	Talk, read, or sing to the bump—your voice now helps build early emotional connections.
The little one's stronger and more frequent movements signal their growing strength and space in the womb.	As the baby grows, noticeable body changes and possible aches reflect her ongoing adaptation to pregnancy.	Assist with chores and optimize comfort at home to ease her increasing physical discomfort.

Week 16 is a blend of new sensory experiences and physical developments, setting the stage for more dynamic interactions between you, your partner, and your little one. Enjoy this exciting time as you continue to engage with your baby's growing abilities and support your partner through the ongoing changes. Keep the tunes loving, the environment comforting, and the vibe positive as you dance through the second trimester!

5.5 WEEK 17: INSULATION INSTALLATION

Welcome to Week 17 of the "Great Pregnancy Playlist!" Strap in because it's time for your baby to put on their winter coat—in the form of adorable (and highly functional) body fat. Meanwhile, the backstage preparations (a.k.a. mommy's body) are ramping up with a curious mix of culinary cravings and the delightful sensation of Braxton Hicks contractions.

Week 17		
Precious Progress	**Maternal Marvels**	**Father's Finesse**
Your baby is now building brown fat, a specialized layer ensuring warmth and energy.	Increased appetite fuels baby growth, accompanied by sporadic Braxton Hicks contractions.	Manage comfort by preparing low-sodium, flavorful snacks and providing soothing foot massages to reduce swelling.
Baby's movements grow stronger as they gain mass, transforming gentle flutters into noticeable wiggles and jabs.	As the baby grows, expect swelling, particularly in the feet and ankles, like unwelcome pregnancy souvenirs.	Track Braxton Hicks contractions to distinguish them from real labor signs, like monitoring beats in a song.

Week 17 is like a bridge in the symphony of pregnancy—connecting the early flutterings with the more robust movements and developments to come. As you and your partner navigate this week, enjoy the interplay of growth, comfort, and preparation. Keep the dialogue open, stay tuned to her needs, and maybe start practicing your swaddling technique on nearby pillows. After all, it's never too early to prepare for the main event!

5.6 WEEK 18: SOUNDCHECK

Welcome to Week 18 of the "What to Expect When Everything is Unexpected" tour! If you thought the first act was a whirlwind of hormones and odd cravings, wait until you see what's next. Buckle up because we're diving into the symphony of your baby's auditory developments. And oh, there might be some unexpected belly concerto performances by your partner, courtesy of the infamous Braxton Hicks contractions.

Week 18		
Precious Progress	**Maternal Marvels**	**Father's Finesse**
Your baby's ears are tuned to hear Mom's heartbeat and voice, preparing for a lifetime of sounds.	These "practice contractions" or Braxton Hicks are dry runs for labor, often causing confusion over whether it's the real deal.	Act as DJ, playing soothing tunes of comfort and support and providing physical relief like back rubs.
The baby's movements are stronger and more frequent, like an active rehearsal for future acrobatics.	An expanding uterus causes more back pain, stretching, and frequent urination, intensifying physical discomfort.	Teach and track Braxton Hicks' signs to differentiate from actual labor, reducing unnecessary panic.

As you groove through Week 18, remember that every kick, sound, and contraction is part of this incredible live performance leading to your baby's big debut. Keep the vibe positive and the support strong, and maybe keep a bag packed because you never know when the real show might kickoff. Enjoy this mix of melodies and movements, and keep tuning in to the needs of your leading lady and your soon-to-be superstar!

5.7 WEEK 19: COATING BABY IN COMFORT

Roll up to Week 19 of the Great Pregnancy Carnival, where your baby decides to don their first superhero cape—or, in utero terms, their first layer of vernix caseosa. Yes, this week, your baby gets slicked up in a creamy, cheese-like substance that's more functional than fashionable. Meanwhile, mommy might start feeling like she's auditioning for a role as a water balloon, thanks to the ever-so-glamorous swelling or edema.

Week 19		
Precious Progress	**Maternal Marvels**	**Father's Finesse**
Your baby is coated in vernix caseosa, like waterproof sunscreen, protecting their skin in the womb.	Mom might see more swelling in her ankles and wrists, a common but cumbersome part of pregnancy.	Encourage her to drink plenty of water to help reduce swelling.
Alongside getting their protective coat, your baby's muscles and bones strengthen, making movements feel stronger.	Her growing belly brings more aches and pains, reminiscent of carrying a lively kickboxing baby.	Offer foot massages, prepare low-salt meals, and consider comfy footwear to ease her growing discomforts.

Week 19 is a mixed bag of slick, superhero skin prep for the baby and a bit of bloating ballet for mom. It's about managing the new developments with a touch of humor and a lot of care. Keep the spirits high and the water flowing, and keep a spare pair of comfy slippers nearby for her. Remember, every step (or waddle) taken is one step closer to meeting the little champion you both are eagerly waiting for. Here's to more growth, laughs, and preparing for the grand entrance!

5.8 WEEK 20: HALFTIME SHOW

Welcome to the halftime show of your pregnancy—Week 20! That's right, you've officially hit the middle mark. This week, it's less about balloon animals and more about real-life baby gymnastics as you catch a detailed glimpse of your little performer during the all-important anatomy scan. Buckle up because it's like front-row tickets to the coolest 4D movie where the star is your tiny human!

Week 20		
Precious Progress	**Maternal Marvels**	**Father's Finesse**
It's time for the detailed anatomy scan, which checks everything from the heart to the toes. Think of it as a comprehensive baby blueprint check.	This might be the week your partner feels the baby move, a reassuring sign of a healthy, active baby.	Be engaged during the anatomy scan. Ask questions, learn, and bond over the real-time images of your developing baby.
Your baby's movements are now more noticeable.	Increased blood volume and pressure on veins can lead to varicose veins and swelling in the legs and feet.	Help your partner enjoy and respond to the baby's kicks. It's a unique way to strengthen their bond.

Week 20 is a significant milestone, filled with excitement, reassurance, and maybe a bit of relief as you pass the halfway point. Enjoy this special preview of your baby's development, and take the time to appreciate how far you've come. It's a blend of medical marvels, physical changes, and emotional highs that make this week a blockbuster hit in your pregnancy journey. Keep up the support, stay engaged, and maybe start thinking about names—if you haven't already. After all, the second act is just about to begin, and it's promising to be as thrilling as the first!

5.9 WEEK 21: GUT FEELINGS

Welcome to Week 21! Strap in for a culinary rollercoaster because this week, your baby's taste buds are officially online, and they're ready to sample whatever gourmet (or not-so-gourmet) dishes mommy decides to indulge in. Imagine your baby as a tiny food critic, silently judging your partner's meals from the comfort of the amniotic fluid. Meanwhile, mommy might notice those cute baby movements turning into full-blown dance routines as your little one gets stronger and more active.

Week 21		
Precious Progress	**Maternal Marvels**	**Father's Finesse**
Baby's taste buds are maturing; they now taste flavors from the amniotic fluid influenced by mom's meals.	More pronounced baby movements make pregnancy feel more real and interactive, though sudden jabs may startle.	Help prepare diverse, nutritious meals to influence the baby's developing palate with healthy flavors.
Baby's movements evolve from gentle flutters to assertive kicks as they grow stronger and respond to different flavors.	Increased baby activity may cause discomfort as space tightens; changes in appetite may introduce new cravings or aversions.	Adapt home comforts; think pregnancy pillows and soothing rubs.

Week 21 is about sensory experiences and preparing for the more dynamic weeks ahead. Enjoy the process of helping your baby develop a taste for the good stuff, and keep supporting your partner as she navigates the ever-changing landscape of pregnancy. It's a time for culinary adventures, comfort adjustments, and interaction with your increasingly active little one. So keep the snacks handy, the comfort high, and your sense of humor ready because each week brings its own set of surprises on this incredible journey!

5.10 WEEK 22: GESTATIONAL GYMNASTICS

Welcome to Week 22, when your baby has turned the womb into a gymnastics arena! As your little one flexes and flips, refining its motor skills, this week also brings new developments for mom, whose role as the nurturer is becoming more physically demanding yet equally fascinating.

Week 22		
Precious Progress	**Maternal Marvels**	**Father's Finesse**
Stronger, coordinated movements during active periods enhance neurological connections and muscle strength.	Mom's appetite increases to meet the nutritional demands of her growing baby.	Promote hydration and a low-sodium diet rich in fruits and vegetables to alleviate swelling and support health.
Baby's movements refine their motor skills and prepare them for post-birth physicality, like astronaut training for zero gravity.	Noticeable swelling helps prepare for childbirth by retaining fluids, especially in the extremities.	Elevate her feet for relief and encourage gentle exercises like walking or swimming to improve circulation.

Week 22 is a dynamic chapter in your pregnancy journey, filled with physical challenges and remarkable developments. As your baby practices prenatal gymnastics and your partner navigates the complexities of her changing body, remember that each step brings you closer to meeting your new family member. Embrace these changes with enthusiasm and care, ensuring that both mom and baby receive the support and love they need to thrive during these transformative weeks.

5.11 WEEK 23: BLOODLINE BEGINS

Welcome to Week 23! As we dive deeper into the second trimester, your baby's bone marrow is taking a significant step forward in its role as the chief blood cell factory. Meanwhile, it's a crucial time for your partner, too, as she undergoes screening for gestational diabetes—an essential health check that ensures both she and the baby are on track for a healthy pregnancy.

Week 23		
Precious Progress	**Maternal Marvels**	**Father's Finesse**
Bone marrow starts producing blood cells this week, taking over from the liver to boost the baby's immune system.	Your partner undergoes glucose screening to monitor her sugar processing.	Provide comfort and support during glucose screening to ease any stress.
This marrow produces essential blood cells that enhance oxygen transport, disease resistance, and healing capabilities.	The growing belly and shifting center of gravity can lead to back pain and discomfort.	If gestational diabetes is diagnosed, prepare balanced meals to maintain healthy blood sugar levels.

Week 23 is a pivotal time filled with crucial developments for both baby and mom. As the baby's bone marrow ramps up to support its growth, your partner faces essential health screenings that will influence the course of the rest of the pregnancy. By staying supportive, engaged, and proactive, you are laying a foundation for a healthy and joyful continuation of this incredible journey towards parenthood. Each step forward, each test, and each meal is part of a larger effort to ensure the well-being of your growing family. Embrace these roles with care and commitment as you prepare for all the exciting developments yet to come.

5.12 WEEK 24: BREATH OF LIFE

Week 24		
Precious Progress	**Maternal Marvels**	**Father's Finesse**
The baby is starting to establish sleep-wake cycles, and periods of activity may alternate with rest.	The growing baby causes increased backaches due to extra weight and shifted center of gravity impacting the spine.	Implement gentle back massages to alleviate discomfort and enhance emotional connection.
Your baby produces surfactant, a substance vital for keeping lung air sacs (alveoli) open after birth.	Numerous body adjustments occur, such as stretching the abdomen, changing posture, and experiencing discomfort in usual sleeping.	Optimize sleeping conditions with a pregnancy pillow to support alignment and relieve back and hip strain.

Welcome to Week 24, a pivotal moment in your pregnancy journey! As your baby meticulously prepares for its first breath, the complexity of its development reaches new heights with the maturation of its respiratory system. This week, we explore the incredible advancements in your baby's lungs and the adaptive changes your partner is experiencing as her body supports this growing life.

As you navigate Week 24, the symphony of development and adaptation continues. Your baby is getting ready to take their first breaths, thanks to their complex respiratory system growth. At the same time, your partner adjusts to the physical demands of her transforming body. Your role as a supportive partner is more crucial than ever—providing comfort, ensuring a soothing environment, and preparing together for the upcoming arrival of your new family member. This week underscores the intricate dance of growth and support that defines the pregnancy journey, highlighting the beauty and challenge of preparing for life's next big breath.

5.13 WEEK 25: FEELING THE FEEDBACK

Week 25		
Precious Progress	**Maternal Marvels**	**Father's Finesse**
Your baby now perceives and responds to external stimuli—sounds, light, touch—reacting to conversations, laughter, and sunlight.	Visible baby movements deepen emotional connections, making the pregnancy a more tangible and shared journey.	Stimulate baby's senses with soft music or gentle belly taps to enhance auditory skills and interactive bonding.
Hair may start to grow on the baby's head, and the body is covered in fine hair called lanugo.	As the uterus expands, it can press against the diaphragm, leading to a feeling of breathlessness.	Help research baby products, birthing plans, and parenting techniques to share the load of preparations.

Week 25 marks a captivating phase in your pregnancy journey, during which the womb becomes an interactive playground. At this stage, every external stimulus from the world outside translates into a sensory response from your baby, turning routine interactions into fascinating dialogues. Your baby is now fine-tuning its senses, actively engaging with the rhythms and nuances of life beyond the womb.

As you venture through Week 25, embrace this stage's dynamic and interactive nature. Each response from your baby, whether a kick in reaction to a melody or a squirm from a flash of light, is an incredible aspect of their development and a step closer to understanding their personality and preferences. This week is about more than just growth; it's about connection, interaction, and the deepening bond forming through every touch, sound, and ray of light. Celebrate and engage in this magical time as you prepare to welcome your baby into the world with love and joy.

5.14 WEEK 26: EYES ON THE PRIZE

Week 26		
Precious Progress	**Maternal Marvels**	**Father's Finesse**
Baby's eyelids are fluttering open, introducing them to light and stimulating visual brain functions for cognitive development.	Your partner may feel more tired due to the physical demands of pregnancy and the need for more rest.	Promote gentle exercises like walking or prenatal yoga and ensure she stays hydrated and rested to minimize discomfort from contractions.
The introduction of light as eyelids open aids visual recognition abilities, which is crucial for post-birth response to stimuli.	Hormonal changes continue to cause mood swings and emotional fluctuations.	Implement relaxation practices like deep breathing, warm baths, or meditation to alleviate contraction discomfort and reduce stress.

Week 26 brings visually and physically exciting developments as your journey through pregnancy continues. Your baby begins to experience their first perceptions of light, marking a significant milestone in their sensory development. At the same time, your partner may start to feel the initial rehearsals for labor with Braxton Hicks contractions.

As you navigate through Week 26, celebrate the milestones and manage the challenges with knowledge and support. The visual developments in your baby are exciting glimpses into their capabilities and the life they will soon experience outside the womb. Simultaneously, understanding and addressing the symptoms of Braxton Hicks contractions prepare both of you for the journey toward labor. This week is about adaptation and anticipation, reinforcing the bond and the shared journey of preparing for the arrival of your new family member. Embrace these developments with excitement and care as you move closer to meeting your baby.

5.15 WEEK 27: GREY MATTER MATTERS

Week 27		
Precious Progress	**Maternal Marvels**	**Father's Finesse**
Brain development enhances neuron networks, which are crucial for future cognitive functions like memory and attention.	Breasts prepare for milk production, expand ducts, and adjust hormones for post-delivery lactation.	Focus on a diet rich in Omega-3 and iron—think salmon, walnuts, and spinach—to boost the baby's brain development.
Brain growth now lays the foundation for processing sensory inputs and future learning.	Breast sensitivity and fullness may cause discomfort.	Ensure she stays hydrated to support amniotic fluid levels and increase blood volume for delivery and lactation.

Week 27 is a transformative period in your pregnancy journey, during which significant neurological advancements occur. As your baby's brain rapidly develops complex neural networks, its capacity for future learning and sensory processing is being established. Concurrently, your partner's body prepares for the crucial role of nourishment post-birth, with specific changes geared towards breastfeeding.

As you progress through the week, the focus is on supporting these profound developments through thoughtful nutrition, hydration, and emotional support. The groundwork laid now is critical for your baby's cognitive abilities and your partner's readiness to nourish and nurture post-birth. This week is about preparation and adaptation, ensuring both the baby's and the mother's bodies are optimally ready for the challenges and joys ahead. Embrace this critical phase with care, ensuring that both mother and baby have what they need to thrive in this incredible journey towards childbirth and beyond.

CHAPTER 6
THE PUSH PLAYBOOK:
STRATEGIES FOR A SMOOTH DELIVERY

I magine it's game day, and you're the coach with the playbook that will guide your team—only not to a touchdown—but through the pulsating, scream-filled arena of the delivery room. Trust me, it's a league where 'overtime' means something completely different, and the right game plan can be the difference between a smooth pass and a fumble on the one-yard line.

6.1 CHOOSING THE RIGHT BIRTH PLAN FOR YOUR FAMILY

Understanding Birth Plan Options

Choosing a birth plan is like choosing the right play in the big game. Each option offers advantages, from the traditional play of natural birth to the strategic maneuver of a cesarean section. Picture a natural birth as the old-school ground-and-pound offense—gritty and intense. Then there's the water birth; think of it as the West Coast offense—more fluid and potentially less painful, offering a soothing environment akin to your team's home-field advantage. And for those situations where a quick change in strategy is crucial, the cesarean section is like the unexpected quarterback sneak, necessary when conditions call for a swift and safe delivery.

Communicating with Healthcare Providers

As the father, you are crucial in communicating with healthcare providers. Just like a quarterback needs to communicate with his coaches, you must ensure your partner's healthcare providers are in sync with your birth plan. It's not just about calling plays from the playbook; it's about discussing options, understanding risks, and ensuring your partner's and baby's health are the top priorities. You are the advocate, sometimes even the linebacker, ensuring the defensive line holds. Ensure that every preference, from pain management to birthing positions, is communicated clearly—like a quarterback relaying audibles to his teammates.

Inclusion of Preferences

Including your preferences in your birth plan is like tailoring your team's playbook to fit your players' individual strengths and needs. Whether it's choosing to have skin-to-skin contact right after birth —a move that helps with early bonding and can be as emotionally satisfying as a touchdown—or selecting the proper method of pain management, each decision should be made to ensure the safety and comfort of your most valuable player, your partner. These preferences are your offensive line; they protect and support your main player through every contraction.

Flexibility and Contingencies

Just like in a game, a good coach will always tell you that even the best game plans need to be able to change. Labor and delivery are no different. It's like a game where the lead can change in seconds. You need a plan that can change at a moment's notice. That might mean going from man-to-man to zone to protect the mother and baby if something goes wrong. Prepare for these changes by discussing what might happen if there is an emergency C-section or if the pain management strategy needs to be altered. Remember, flexibility and adaptability can be the key to a successful delivery.

Communicating with Healthcare Providers

Let's circle back to communication—it's that important. Think of your healthcare providers as the special teams. They come in at key points and can make a big difference. Good communication here means making sure they know what's in your birth plan and why. It means making sure they respect your partner's wishes and follow through with the delivery as planned. Everyone needs to be on the same page, whether it's a routine or trick play. Rest assured, they are there to support you and your partner every step of the way.

The Birth Plan Playbook

Consider this link to be a visual cheat sheet like those wristbands quarterbacks wear to remember plays. It's a detailed, clear template for your birth plan choices, preferences for pain management, and contingency strategies. This template can be a quick reference for you, your partner, and the healthcare team during the hectic moments of labor and delivery, ensuring everyone knows the game plan and can execute it as smoothly as possible. Visit the link at https://thebump-doc.s3.amazonaws.com/birth_plan.pdf or scan the QR code below.

In this chapter of your fatherhood playbook, understanding the various plays at your disposal and how to effectively communicate them ensures you're ready to lead your family to a winning delivery at game time. Remember, the goal here isn't just to reach the end zone; it's to make the journey there as rewarding and safe as possible for your partner and new baby. So, call those plays with confidence, coach!

6.2 UNDERSTANDING THE ROLE OF HEALTHCARE PROFESSIONALS

Think of childbirth as building a team for a big game. You have your coach, players, and fans. In childbirth, your team is made up of different medical professionals, each with their own expertise.

Midwives: The Tactical Coordinators

Midwives are like the special teams coordinators, experts in managing the game under normal circumstances. They specialize in childbirth and reproductive health, providing care through the prenatal period, during labor, and postpartum. Picture them as your day-to-day contact, guiding you through the normal processes of pregnancy and childbirth with a focus on low-intervention strategies. Their approach is hands-on and personal, like a coach who knows his players individually and tailors strategies to their strengths. Midwives are trained to handle uncomplicated deliveries and are adept at recognizing when complications arise, at which point they collaborate with obstetricians—think of them calling in the quarterback when a specialized play is needed. They come in different types: Certified Nurse Midwives (CNMs), Certified Midwives (CMs), and Certified Professional Midwives (CPMs), each with specific training but all with the same goal: a safe and healthy delivery.

Doulas: The Ultimate Support Squad

Doulas are like cheerleaders and personal trainers, all wrapped into one. They don't do the medical stuff, but they're still important. They give emotional and physical support throughout labor, helping to manage pain and comfort with things like breathing and labor positioning. Imagine having a coach there to keep you going, keep your spirits up, and make sure you stick to the plan. Doulas works with the medical staff to ensure your partner's preferences are heard, and her needs are met. They've been shown to reduce labor times and the need for medical interventions. It's like having an expert who can help you avoid unnecessary penalties and keep the game moving.

Obstetricians (OB/GYNs): The High-Stakes Players

Obstetricians are like the head coaches in high-stakes playoff games. They specialize in pregnancy, childbirth, and the postpartum period and step in when specialized medical care is needed. They manage high-risk pregnancies and perform surgical interventions, such as cesarean sections, when necessary. Their role is critical in ensuring the health and safety of both mother and baby, especially when complications arise that require immediate and expert medical intervention. Think of them as making tough calls under pressure; ensuring the team's safety is always the priority.

Anesthesiologists: The Pain Management Experts

No one likes pain, and in the childbirth arena, anesthesiologists are the go-to professionals for managing it. They're the special ops of pain relief, skilled in administering epidurals and other forms of anesthesia that help manage pain during labor. Their expertise is not just about comfort; it's about ensuring that the mother can focus on the task at hand—delivering the baby—without the distraction of overwhelming pain. They play a crucial role in the team, ready to adjust their strategies based on how the labor progresses and address any anesthesia-related complications.

Nurses: The Frontline Caregivers

Labor and delivery nurses are like unsung heroes, the offensive linemen who are always on the front lines, providing continuous care. They monitor the health of the mother and the baby, assist with pain management, and support the birthing plan. Their role is hands-on and essential, offering the support needed to navigate through each phase of labor. They are often the primary caregivers, providing the necessary link between the family and the different specialists, ensuring communication and care are seamless and practical.

These professionals play a vital role in the childbirth experience, ensuring safety, support, and expert care. As a dad-to-be, understanding who is on your team and what they do can make you an informed and proactive participant in your child's birth. Remember, while you may not be the one catching the baby at the end zone, your support and understanding of each player's role can make a significant difference in the smooth delivery of your newest team member.

6.3 PACKING THE HOSPITAL BAG: A DAD'S CHECKLIST

Let's be real; you can't just throw a few things in a bag and call it good when you're getting ready to go to the hospital. This is the real deal, the big show, the "packing for the arrival of your new family member" kind of deal. And just like a good scout, you need to have your bag packed with your essentials and those of your MVP (Most Valuable Partner) and the soon-to-be rookie of the year.

First off, let's talk about the essentials for mom and baby. Think of this as packing for the star player and the new recruit. For your partner, it's all about comfort and practicality. Pack things like a comfortable robe and slippers, a couple of maternity outfits, and all the necessary toiletries. And don't forget the important stuff like your birth plan documents, insurance info, and ID. You'll want your baby's first outfit (yes, the coming home outfit), swaddles, and newborn diapers. Keep in mind that hospitals usually provide some basics like diapers and wipes, but it's good to have your own, just in case.

Moving onto your gear – because, let's be honest, you need to be in top form too. Pack snacks, lots and lots of snacks. You don't want your stomach growling during the key moments. Comfortable clothes are a must, and maybe throw in a sweatshirt because hospital temperatures can fluctuate more wildly than a rookie's first-game nerves. Add a charger for your devices, a good book, or your tablet for those potential long waits, and why not a pillow? Your comfort is key in maintaining the stamina to support your partner through the marathon that is labor.

Now, comfort items for your partner can be a game-changer. These could range from her favorite pillow (because hospital pillows can feel like they're stuffed with thin air) to a playlist of her favorite tunes or a calming scent like lavender. These items might seem small, but they can be as crucial as that clutch field goal kick at the game's finish. They help create a more personal and soothing environment, which can be a tremendous comfort during labor.

Last-minute items can often be the most forgotten. Make a list of what to grab on your way out. This could be anything from her glasses to a contact lens kit or a quick snack. Just ensure it's somewhere obvious, like on the fridge or door, so it's the last thing you see before leaving.

Packing the hospital bag may not be glamorous, but it's important. It's about ensuring you, the coach, and your star players are ready to handle the big day. With everything packed, you can focus on what's important – supporting your partner and meeting your baby for the first time.

As you finish this chapter, remember that packing is more than just throwing things into a bag. It's about ensuring you're ready to support your partner through one of the most significant moments of your lives. It's about making sure you're not running around at the last minute but can instead focus on the task at hand. Later, we'll discuss what to do when you get to the hospital and spend the first few hours with your new baby so you're packed and prepared for the day.

CHAPTER 7
NURSERY KNOW-HOW:
DAD'S GUIDE TO ESSENTIAL BABY GEAR

Imagine transforming a blank canvas into a masterpiece of comfort and style. Except this time, the canvas is your baby's nursery, and you're the artist equipped with cribs instead of paintbrushes. Setting up the nursery is like gearing up for the most epic tailgate party, where the guest of honor is your new baby. It's all about creating a safe, soothing, and stimulating environment where your little MVP will kick off their life's adventure. So, grab your tool belt – it's time to build a little nest that's as functional as it is cozy.

7.1 SETTING UP THE NURSERY: A DAD'S CHECKLIST

Essential Nursery Items

Let's start with the basics. Think of this as your packing list for an expedition into the wilds of parenthood. First up, the sleeping quarters: a sturdy crib that meets all current safety standards. Remember, this little bed needs to be the Fort Knox of cribs – solid, safe, and without old-school drop sides. A firm mattress that fits snugly within the crib ensures no gaps could become potential hazards.

Next, you'll need sheets – but not just any sheets. Go for fitted ones that won't bunch up around your baby, creating a smooth, safe sleeping surface. Now, while we're on the subject of sleep, a sound machine can be a game-changer. It's like having a white noise linebacker blocking out the chaos of the outside world to help your rookie get some quality shut-eye.

Storage is your next key player. A good dresser can double as a changing table if you secure a changing pad on top, making it a versatile piece in your nursery lineup. And let's not forget a comfortable yet durable rocking chair. Whether you're cuddling, feeding, or enjoying quiet moments, this chair will be your best buddy in the wee hours.

Safety Considerations

Now, onto the defense strategy – baby-proofing. Every outlet needs a cover – think of them as little helmets protecting your curious tyke from electrical blitzes. Keep all cords out of reach; baby's exploration shouldn't lead to a tangle with danger. Secure furniture to the walls – dressers and bookshelves can look like Mount Everest to a tiny climber, so strap them down to prevent any climbing mishaps.

Another strategic play is the crib's location. Keep it away from windows, blinds, and curtains to avoid entanglements or drafts. This positioning also reduces the risk of your baby pulling anything down onto themselves as they grow and become more mobile.

Creating a Comfortable Environment

Setting the right ambiance in the nursery is like adjusting the stadium lights for the big game – it makes all the difference. Soft, ambient lighting is key; a dimmable lamp or nightlight provides enough glow for midnight diaper changes without disrupting the cozy, sleepy vibe.

Temperature control is crucial. You want your little champ to be comfortable, not too hot or cold. A room thermometer can help keep the nursery at a comfy 68-72 degrees Fahrenheit. As for noise levels, that sound machine will help drown out disruptive noises, from street traffic to household clatter, ensuring your baby isn't jolted awake by an unexpected noise penalty.

Involvement in Decoration

Now it's time to have fun and let the interior designer in you loose. Decorating the nursery isn't just about making the room look nice; it's about connecting with the space where you'll be nursing your baby, changing their diapers, and watching them grow. Choose a theme you and your partner like, such as an adventure theme or something more calming like a botanical theme, and paint the walls, add decals, and hang up art that makes you feel good.

Make sure your partner is involved in picking things out and arranging the room. That way, you'll both feel connected to the space and be able to picture what life will be like with your new baby. It's like drawing up a playbook and making sure everyone knows the plays.

7.2 MUST-HAVE GEAR FOR THE FIRST SIX MONTHS

Navigating the baby gear landscape is like picking the right tools for a camping trip in the wilderness. You need reliable equipment that won't give out on you when it matters most. For the first six months, your kit needs to be well-equipped yet not overflowing; it's about finding that sweet spot between necessity and luxury. Let's break down the real MVPs (Most Valuable Products) in each category: cribs, car seats, strollers, and baby carriers, helping you select gear that scores high on safety, functionality, and dad-friendly usability.

Deciphering between the must-haves and the nice-to-haves starts with the basics: the crib is your baby's home base. You need a sturdy crib that meets all current safety certifications. While design and aesthetics are a plus, the focus should be on structural integrity and the absence of small parts that could become hazards. Next are car seats– your baby's safety harness on the road. You want a new, high-rated car seat that fits your vehicle correctly and offers easy installation. Many new models have bases that remain in the car, allowing the seat to click in and out easily – an absolute back-saver when you need to move a sleeping baby.

Strollers are your next big ticket item. Consider your terrain and lifestyle. Are you navigating city sidewalks or country roads? Do you need something lightweight for quick trips or a more robust model to handle trails and longer walks? Look for models with adjustable handles so both tall and short parents can stroll comfortably, ample storage for those baby essentials, and an easy-fold mechanism to avoid any parking lot wrestling matches.

Lastly, baby carriers are about keeping your little one close and your hands free. It's about comfort for you and your baby, so look for carriers with good lumbar support and adjustable straps. A versatile carrier that adjusts as your baby grows and can be worn in various positions will give you the best bang for your buck.

Feeding Necessities

Whether you're championing the breast or the bottle, having the right gear can make all the difference when it comes to feeding. For breastfeeding, a reliable breast pump is essential for any mom planning to pump at work or even for those occasional nights out. Look for a model that's both efficient and gentle, with adjustable settings to match comfort levels. Storage solutions for pumped milk are just as crucial—opt for BPA-free storage bags or containers that seal tightly and stack easily in the fridge or freezer.

Bottle-feeding dads, you're up at bat here, too. A selection of bottles designed to reduce air intake can help prevent colic and discomfort during feeding. Babies can be picky about their bottles, so try a few different types before buying in bulk. And don't forget a high-quality bottle sterilizer and warmer to keep things squeaky clean and just the right temperature.

Sleeping Arrangements

Sleep is a precious commodity in any new parent's world. Creating the perfect sleep environment starts with choosing the right sleeping gear. A bassinet can be a great first bed for your baby, offering a cozy, compact space that fits conveniently next to your bed for those first few months. Look for one with a stable base and breathable sides. As your baby grows, transitioning to a crib is the next step. Ensure the crib mattress is firm, fits snugly within the crib frame, and keep it free of toys and accessories (this includes blankets and pillows) that could pose a risk.

Health and Grooming

No parent should have to scramble to find the right tools for health and grooming. A well-stocked first aid kit for babies should include essentials like a digital thermometer, nasal aspirator, and a baby-friendly saline solution. For grooming, invest in a good set of baby nail clippers or files—those little nails are sharper than they look and require regular trimming to prevent scratches.

Each piece of gear you choose is like selecting the right player for your team; it needs to fit into your game plan seamlessly and perform under pressure, whether that's a middle-of-the-night feeding or a stroll through the park. Choose wisely, and you'll find that these essentials make life easier and enhance those precious moments with your new baby.

UNLOCK THE POWER OF GENEROSITY

"The best way to find yourself is to lose yourself in the service of others."

MAHATMA GANDHI.

Hey there, Dad-to-Be! Helping others makes you feel great and can make a big difference in the lives of others. If we've got a chance to improve someone's life during our time together, I say let's go for it!

So, here's the question:

Would you help someone you've never met, even if you never got credit for it?

This person is just like you. Or, at least, like you used to be. A first-time dad riding the emotional rollercoaster, looking for advice and guidance but unsure where to find it.

Our mission is to make the journey to fatherhood easier and more enjoyable for every Dad-to-Be. And the only way to reach everyone is with your help.

Most people do, in fact, judge a book by its cover (and its reviews). So here's my ask on behalf of a fellow Dad-to-Be you've never met:

Please help that new dad by leaving this book a review.

Your review costs nothing and takes less than 60 seconds, but it could change a fellow dad's life forever. Your review could help…

- one more dad feel ready for fatherhood.
- one more partner feel supported.
- one more family start strong.
- one more baby, get a confident, loving dad.

To get that 'feel good' feeling and help this person, all you have to do is leave a review.

★★★★★ RATE

If you feel good about helping a fellow dad, you're one of us. Welcome to the club!

Scan the below QR code to leave a review:

https://www.amazon.com/review/create-review/?asin=
B0DKSQCDCP

I'm super excited to help you become the best dad you can be faster and easier than you can imagine. You'll love the tips, stories, and strategies in the coming chapters. Thank you from the bottom of my heart. Now, let's dive back in!

- *Your biggest fan, Collin Web*

CollinWebb

PS - Fun fact: Helping others makes you feel great and boosts your own happiness. If you think this book will help another Dad-to-Be, pass it on!

CHAPTER 8
FROM BUMP TO BABY:
3RD TRIMESTER

You're in the final quarter of the big game; the score is tight, and the clock is ticking down. Welcome to the third trimester, my friend, where every week brings you closer to the moment you've been training for fatherhood. This isn't just any countdown. It's a meticulously timed preparation for one of life's most awe-inspiring halftime shows—birth.

8.1 WEEK 28: BUTTERBALL BABY

Welcome to the third trimester, when your baby prepares to exit the cozy, rent-free accommodation of the womb, and your partner turns into a walking, talking (and sometimes grunting) bundle of nerves and excitement. It's a thrilling time packed with anticipation and a fair share of 'oh boy, what now?' moments. Strap in, Dad. It will be a wild ride filled with wonders and wobbles.

Week 28		
Precious Progress	**Maternal Marvels**	**Father's Finesse**
Your baby now focuses on fat accumulation to regulate body temperature after birth.	Practice contractions help prepare the body for labor despite being mildly annoying.	Ensure home comfort with pillows, snacks, and hydration; respect her temperature preferences.
The baby's brain is in its final development stages, getting smarter every day.	Hormonal changes can cause rapid emotional swings from euphoria to tears.	Learn signs of preterm labor and health markers.
Movements become more pronounced as the baby gets stronger and space gets tighter.	The urge to clean and organize intensifies, driven by her nesting instinct.	Help with nesting by painting, assembling furniture, and fulfilling cravings.

As the due date approaches, remember that every bizarre craving, every midnight grunt, and every single inexplicable tear is part of the incredible journey to meet your new little human. Keep your humor handy, your patience plentiful, and your support unwavering. Get ready to cheer, support, and shed a tear or two yourself. It's the most exhilarating 'game' you'll ever be part of—prepare to play your heart out until you hear that magical first cry. Game on, Dad!

8.2 WEEK 29: THE GREAT STRETCH

Buckle up, Dad, because your baby and partner are both entering a growth spurt that makes the last season of your favorite TV show look tame. Your home is about to feel more like a sports arena during playoffs, with your partner as the star player gearing up for the big day—minus the hot dogs and overpriced beer.

FROM BUMP TO BABY: 91

Week 29		
Precious Progress	**Maternal Marvels**	**Father's Finesse**
The baby is gaining mass, which is crucial for warmth and energy after birth.	Baby's growth rearranges organs, making comfort a luxury.	Use pillows strategically for your partner's comfort
Baby's movements increase, causing visible belly ripples.	Finding a comfortable sleep position becomes challenging due to the baby's size and movements.	Establish calming pre-sleep rituals like back rubs or warm baths.
Baby's bones are hardening, preparing for the outside world.	Increased bathroom trips as the baby presses on the bladder.	Assist with late-night bathroom trips and cravings.

As you approach the two-minute warning, remember that every growth spurt, every restless night, and every belly kick is a sign of the amazing journey you are both on. It's a time filled with anticipation, a fair bit of discomfort, and incredible transformation. Keep your sense of humor ready, your support unwavering, and your heart open. You're not just spectators in this game; you're key players in the most important match of your lives. Cheer loud, support hard, and get ready to meet your newest teammate soon. Let the final countdown begin!

8.3 WEEK 30: SHAKE, RATTLE, AND ROLL

Welcome to Week 30, where your baby rehearses for an in-womb Olympics. It's all kicks, flips, and wiggles in there as if your little one is putting on a nightly show just for you (minus the admission fee). Get your popcorn ready, Dad, because this active phase means your baby is healthy and growing precisely as it should—though it might feel like she is housing a tiny, energetic gymnast.

Week 30		
Precious Progress	**Maternal Marvels**	**Father's Finesse**
Baby's increased movements develop and refine muscles, bones, joints, reflexes, and nervous system.	Stomach acid causes heartburn due to the baby taking up more room.	Prepare bland meals like oatmeal, bananas, and yogurt.
Baby practices breathing by taking in amniotic fluid.	Shortness of breath increases as the baby presses on the lungs.	Serve small, frequent meals to ease heartburn.
Increased activity enhances the touch and hearing senses.	The physical demands of carrying extra weight, combined with disrupted sleep, can lead to increased fatigue, emotional fluctuations, and anxiety.	Encourage prenatal yoga or meditation for relaxation.

As the third trimester marches on, remember, Dad, your support is as critical as ever. Your partner's body is doing the heavy lifting, but your role in providing comfort, understanding, and a few well-placed pillows can make all the difference. Keep cheering, keep supporting, and keep those bland snacks coming. The finish line is in sight, and you're both doing spectacularly. Let the good times roll as you prepare to welcome your little one into the world with open arms and a heart full of love.

8.4 WEEK 31: SENSE-SATIONAL BABY

Welcome to Week 31 of the great pregnancy saga. This is the week your tiny human decides to fully boot up all their senses, turning the womb into a 4D cinema. Taste, smell, hear, see, and touch—it's all happening now! Imagine your little one tuning into the world from the inside, getting ready for their big reveal. So, prepare your commentary, Dad, because it's about to get interactive!

Week 31		
Precious Progress	**Maternal Marvels**	**Father's Finesse**
Your baby is developing their palette by sampling flavors from Mom's meals.	Your partner feels increased pressure on the lower abdomen as the baby grows.	Do gentle pregnancy-safe exercises together.
Baby starts to smell scents in the amniotic fluid.	Added weight and pressure make movements deliberate.	Encourage swimming or floating to relieve pressure.

As you both ride the waves of this sense-sational phase, remember, every bit of interaction, every meal shared, and every playlist curated isn't just passing the time—it's helping your baby prepare for life outside the womb. Your role as Dad is more crucial than ever, ensuring your partner feels supported and comfortable as she houses your budding sensory scientist. Keep the humor alive, the support constant, and the love flowing. The countdown is on, and every day brings you closer to meeting the newest member of your team. So stay playful, stay prepared, and, as always, stay tuned to Mom and baby's needs. The final whistle is about to blow, and it will be magnificent!

8.5 WEEK 32: SNUG AS A BUG

Welcome to Week 32. Think of it as downsizing from a spacious loft to a charming, yet notably smaller, studio apartment. There's less room for the dance parties and more about strategic shifting. Your baby is now a tiny minimalist, perfecting the art of moving efficiently in increasingly cramped quarters.

Week 32		
Precious Progress	**Maternal Marvels**	**Father's Finesse**
Baby's movements shift to subtle wiggles due to limited space.	Colostrum, the first form of milk, begins production. It's packed with nutrients and antibodies.	Track daily kick counts to monitor the baby's activity patterns.
Movements prepare the baby for navigating the birth canal.	Occasional leaks indicate the body is preparing for nursing.	Maintain communication with healthcare providers if movement patterns change.

As you navigate the cozy confines of Week 32, remember that each wiggle and each drop of colostrum is part of an incredible journey toward the big debut. Your role is to monitor, support, and cheerlead through these snug times. Keep the spirits up and the communication open. You're almost at the finish line, where the reward—a brand new life to cherish and nurture—far outweighs the cramped quarters and sleepless nights. Stay snug, stay smart, and stay excited, Dad. The best is yet to come!

8.6 WEEK 33: BUILDING BABY'S IMMUNE FORT

As you march further into the third trimester, your baby isn't just growing; they're also building a defense system akin to a medieval fortress. Thanks to the wonder of biology, your partner is transferring her elite squad of antibodies to the little one, beefing up their immune system like a coach bolsters a football team's defense line before the big game. This isn't just growth—it's strategic preparation for life outside the cozy castle of the womb.

	Week 33	
Precious Progress	**Maternal Marvels**	**Father's Finesse**
Your baby receives antibodies from Mom. These antibodies provide a temporary immune shield.	Your partner may experience increased swelling in her hands and feet.	Take over physical tasks to ease her load.
Neurons are maturing, and synapses are forming quickly, enhancing the baby's ability to process information and react to stimuli.	General discomfort rises with the baby's increased weight.	Offer emotional support, listen, and maintain positivity. This may sound repetitive at this point, but it's a necessity.

As you both prepare for the arrival of your new team member, remember that every antibody transferred, every pillow adjusted, and every supportive word exchanged is building towards that incredible moment of first contact. You're not just spectators in this; you're active participants in one of life's most incredible adventures. Keep up the humor, stay flexible in your support strategies, and cherish these final weeks. The finish line is in sight and promises the joy of a lifetime. Keep building that fort, Dad, because soon you'll defend it with your newest, tiniest ally. The whistle is about to blow, and it's almost game time!

8.7 WEEK 34: FAT FORTRESS

Week 34		
Precious Progress	**Maternal Marvels**	**Father's Finesse**
Your baby is developing a specialized warmth and energy fat packed with mitochondria, known as "Brown Fat."	Your partner is experiencing increased anxiety as the due date nears, similar to pre-game jitters.	Review birth plan details to turn the unknown into a well-marked map.
This fat production prepares the baby to regulate body temperature independently after birth.	Excitement and nerves create intense emotional swings.	Prepare for various scenarios to reduce anxiety through preparation.

Your tiny emperor is busy constructing their own personal insulation layer, stocking up on brown fat like it's going out of style. This isn't just any fat; it's the Rolls-Royce of baby fat, equipped with mitochondria that act like tiny internal heaters. As you gear up for the grand entrance, think of this fat as the baby's first winter coat, tailor-made by nature to face the brisk world outside the womb.

As you both prepare for the arrival of your bundle of joy, remember that the layers of brown fat your baby is building are matched by the layers of preparation you add each day. These final weeks are about bolstering defenses, fortifying your team spirit, and ensuring the fortress you're building is ready for its new inhabitant. So keep up the support and humor alive, and remember: you're not just preparing for a birth; you're laying the foundation for your family's future. Together, you're invincible—ready to welcome your newest champion into the world with open arms and warm hearts. Let's get fortified!

8.8 WEEK 35: BABY BULK

Week 35		
Precious Progress	**Maternal Marvels**	**Father's Finesse**
Baby continues to gain weight for warmth and energy.	A growing baby increases pressure on organs, causing frequent urination.	Set up a nightlight path and keep essentials handy for nightly bathroom trips.
Baby practices sucking, swallowing, and breathing skills that they'll need from minute one on the outside.	Baby's growth makes movement more challenging and requires planning and effort.	Offer steady support for walking and getting up.

Welcome to Week 35, where your little one is beefing up for their big debut. Consider it the final prep stage before a boxer enters the ring, except cuter and with less violence. Your baby is turning into a pint-sized powerhouse, packing on layers of fat to stay toasty and energized for the big day. It's like they're filling their pockets with snacks for a marathon they never signed up for but are destined to run!

As you both approach the final stretch of this incredible journey, remember that every pound your baby gains and every challenge your partner faces is part of the preparation for a new life about to begin. Your support and involvement are invaluable, transforming you into the MVP of Team Family. Keep up the spirit, maintain the support, and gear up for the grand finale. The final whistle is about to blow, and it will be a game-changer. So stay tuned, stay supportive, and get ready to cheer your hearts out as you welcome your newest little champion into the world!

8.9 WEEK 36: BREATH OF FRESH AIR

Week 36		
Precious Progress	**Maternal Marvels**	**Father's Finesse**
Baby's lungs produce more surfactant, which helps keep those airways open.	Cleaning and organizing intensify to prepare for the baby.	Ensure baby supplies are stocked and organized.
Lungs prepare for the transition from fluid-breathing to air-breathing.	Your partner's excitement and anxiety rise as labor approaches.	Learn labor signs to provide calm, reassuring support.

Welcome to Week 36 in the journey of pregnancy! Your tiny athlete is almost ready for the big league, particularly mastering the art of breathing. Imagine your baby's lungs as two small, high-tech balloons gearing up for their debut inflation once they hit the real world. It's critical as these lungs undergo final checks, ensuring they're slick and ready for that first victorious gulp of air.

As you wrap up the final preparations for the baby's arrival and your partner's comfort, remember that every task completed, every item checked off the list, and every moment spent together in these final weeks are building blocks for your new life as a family. Your baby's first breath will soon fill your world with joy, and your home will transform into a sanctuary of love and care. Keep up the positive energy, cherish these final moments of anticipation, and get ready to welcome the little champion who's about to make a grand entrance into your lives. It's nearly showtime, so let's make these last preparations count!

8.10 WEEK 37: LOCK AND LOAD

Congratulations are in order because your baby has officially reached full-term status! This is the week your little one crosses off all their pre-birth training and checks into the ready-to-launch club. Imagine your baby donning a graduation cap because they're prepared to meet the world anytime. This isn't just a milestone; it's like getting the green light on a race track—your rookie could speed off the starting line any moment now!

Week 37		
Precious Progress	**Maternal Marvels**	**Father's Finesse**
Your baby has reached full term, which means its respiratory and cardiovascular systems are ready for the outside world.	Your partner's cervix dilates and effaces, preparing for childbirth.	Ensure the hospital bag is packed with essentials for Mommy, Daddy, and Baby.
Baby gains about half an ounce daily, storing fat for temperature regulation and energy.	With the baby full-term, every new sensation might indicate the start of labor.	Keep the car fueled and the infant car seat installed correctly.

As you embark on Week 37, embrace the excitement and perhaps a touch of nerves with humor and grace. Your baby is practically at the doorstep, and every preparation you make now is part of welcoming them into the world. Keep your hospital bag by the door, your car keys handy, and your spirit ready for one of life's most transformative experiences. Soon, you'll shift from pregnancy to parenthood, from preparations to action, waiting to welcoming. Get ready to meet your MVP—it's almost game time!

8.11 WEEK 38: READY TO ROLL

Welcome to Week 38. It's like your little racer is in the pit lane, engines revving, getting the final polish before the big race. Every organ, every tiny detail, is being fine-tuned to perfection. This isn't just a pre-launch check; it's the crucial last-minute adjustments before the grand entrance into the world. Think of it as the baby adding racing stripes and checking tire pressure, ready to zoom into your lives.

Week 38		
Precious Progress	**Maternal Marvels**	**Father's Finesse**
Final brain connections optimize your baby's cognitive functions.	The real contractions are setting in—Stronger, frequent contractions prepare for labor.	Ensure her comfort with pillows, hydration, and snacks.
Baby fine-tunes reflexes for immediate post-birth interaction.	The increased physical intensity of contractions brings intense emotional swings.	Track contractions, time them, and assist with breathing techniques.

As you navigate Week 38, remember that every little tweak, every final adjustment, and every moment of support counts. You're both in the homestretch of this amazing race, and the finish line is now in clear sight. Keep your spirits high, your bags packed, and your heart ready to embrace the chaos and joy of meeting your little one. The race is almost over, and your greatest adventure is about to begin.

Stay tuned, stay supportive, and get ready to welcome your newest team member with open arms and a heart full of love.

8.12 WEEK 39: ANY DAY NOW

Imagine you're at the edge of your seat during the final moments of a thriller—every tick of the clock is suspenseful. That's where you are in the pregnancy playbook. Your baby, cozy and fully developed, is just adding some final touches—like a painter on a masterpiece—before making the grand entrance. This isn't just the season finale of your favorite show; it's the premiere of something spectacular: your child's birth.

Week 39		
Precious Progress	**Maternal Marvels**	**Father's Finesse**
Baby moves into the optimal birth position.	Increased baby pressure causes significant discomfort.	Engage in activities to divert her focus from discomfort.
Sucking and grasping reflexes are fine-tuned.	Hormonal surges cause emotional swings.	Double-check the hospital bag, rehearse the route, and prepare for departure.

As you navigate through Week 39, remember that this is more than just a waiting game—it's about cherishing these last moments as a duo before you become a trio. Every day is a step closer to meeting the new love of your lives. So hold her hand, keep up the positive vibes, and stay ready. The final buzzer is about to sound and will be a momentous shift from anticipation to reality. Keep your eyes on the prize, your heart open, and your bag ready. The adventure is about to get even more exciting!

8.13 WEEK 40: IT'S GO TIME!

This is the week where every twitch and twinge might send you scrambling for the hospital bag. It's like being all dressed up with nowhere to go—yet. Your baby, now fully cooked to perfection, might be taking their sweet time making the grand entrance, proving they already have a mind of their own. It's not just game day; it's potentially the biggest debut of your lives!

Week 40		
Precious Progress	**Maternal Marvels**	**Father's Finesse**
Baby fine-tunes vital skills like breathing, sucking, and gripping.	The due date brings excitement, impatience, and anxiety.	Keep the hospital bag ready and know the signs of real labor.
The baby moves deeper into the birth canal, ready for delivery.	Signs of labor include baby "dropping," back pain, and loss of mucus plug.	Reassure her that passing the due date is normal and that medical support is ready.

As you both stand by at Week 40, ready for the action to start, remember that this period of anticipation is just the quiet before the beautiful storm. Every moment of waiting is another moment your baby is using to prepare perfectly for their debut. Keep those spirits up, the bags packed, and those supportive vibes strong. Soon, you'll move from the sidelines to the main event, from preparation to action, from duo to trio. Stay excited, stay supportive, and get ready to meet your new MVP!

8.14 WEEK 41: OVERTIME

Welcome to Week 41: We are officially into overtime! This is the week where patience is tested, and anticipation is at its peak. Think of it as being geared up and ready for kickoff, but the game's been delayed, and the fans are on the edge of their seats. While it might seem like you're just idling by, remember your baby is still getting some final tune-ups—like a race car in the pit before the final lap.

Week 41		
Precious Progress	**Maternal Marvels**	**Father's Finesse**
Even past the due date, your baby gains crucial fat for temperature regulation.	Your partner will attend frequent doctor visits to monitor the baby's growth and ensure a safe delivery.	Keep spirits high with humor and support.
Healthcare staff will monitor the baby's heart rate response to movements.	The growing baby continues to experience increased daily discomfort and fatigue.	Engage in light entertainment to distract her.

Navigating Week 41's overtime is a true test of patience and support. But remember, every additional day your baby spends in the womb is another day they spend getting ready to meet the world in the best shape possible. Keep focusing on the joy that will come, maintain your cheerleader spirit, and prepare for the big day. You're not just waiting but actively participating in these final moments before your life changes wonderfully. So keep up the good spirits, stay engaged, and get ready to welcome your little champ. The final whistle is about to blow, and it will be spectacular!

8.15 WEEK 42: EVICTION NOTICE

Your baby has decided to extend their stay in the womb's luxury suite, and now the medical team is ready to gently suggest it's time to check out. The excitement of the due date has passed, and now, every day feels like you're waiting for a delayed flight to finally take off.

Congratulations, you're in the home stretch, even if it feels like a marathon that just won't end. You're officially in the final phase of pregnancy at 42 weeks—where you can feel the anticipation, excitement, and a healthy dose of impatience. It's like waiting for the star performer to hit the stage while they're still cozy in the green room. While your partner might feel like she's been hosting a long-term guest, this extra time is not wasted. It's building up to one of the most incredible moments of your lives. You've both been troopers, navigating these final days with grace and patience (or as much patience as one can muster when carrying a fully grown baby). The medical team might be talking about induction, and that's okay. It's like hitting the reset button on a game console—it ensures everything starts smoothly when nature needs a nudge.

Week 42		
Precious Progress	**Maternal Marvels**	**Father's Finesse**
The baby is fully developed, adding final fat reserves.	Carrying a full-term-plus baby is physically demanding and uncomfortable.	Understand the induction process to reduce anxiety.
The baby continues to practice breathing, swallowing, and sucking skills.	Waiting for labor can increase anxiety and restlessness.	Ensure the hospital bag is ready and travel plans are set.
The baby makes subtle movements in preparation for birth.	Pre-labor signs include increased cervical dilation, which can contribute to physical and emotional anticipation.	Keep her comfortable with massages, favorite foods, and relaxing activities.

As you prepare for this miraculous moment, know that the end of pregnancy is just the beginning of a new adventure. The grand entrance is imminent, and soon, you'll be welcoming your newest family member, ready to bring joy, chaos, and a whole new kind of love into your lives. Hold on just a bit longer; the finish line is in sight, and the best is yet to come. Welcome to the final play—it's going to be legendary.

CHAPTER 9
DAD'S DELIVERY DUTIES:
DELIVERY ROOM 101

Imagine you're prepping for the ultimate DIY project, but instead of a YouTube tutorial, you have a room full of medical professionals. Instead of building a bookshelf, you're bringing a baby into the world. Welcome to the delivery room, where your baby will make their debut. This isn't just any day at the DIY shop —this is the big league of fatherhood, and you're about to play a pivotal role.

9.1 UNDERSTANDING THE STAGES OF LABOR FROM A DAD'S PERSPECTIVE

Recognizing Labor Signs

Alright, you think you're prepared? The first thing you need to know is when labor is starting. It's like knowing when the pizza is about to arrive, except you're not waiting for a pizza, and there's a lot more yelling. Early labor signs can be as subtle as your partner's mood swings or as obvious as her water breaking, which isn't always the big splash you see in the movies. Sometimes it's just a trickle.

I remember when I got a text from my wife near the end of a sixteen-hour shift, saying, "I think my water broke." Of course, I called her immediately and asked, "You think, or you know?" It wasn't like the movies at all. After we confirmed her water had broken, I made the 45-minute drive in about 20 minutes, and I expected to find her in the middle of labor and in a lot of pain. Instead, I walked in to find her at the sink doing the dishes. We grabbed our bags and headed to the hospital.

Contractions are another sign to watch for. Differentiating them from Braxton-Hicks is important. If I had known the discomfort my wife was feeling the previous day was actual contractions, I would have taken the day off. These contractions can feel like a regular tightening or cramping across the belly. Every woman is different, but these can start as mild discomfort and progress through the stages of labor. Timing these contractions is your first official duty. Use that stopwatch app you usually reserve to grill steaks. When these contractions are coming at regular intervals and getting stronger, it's time to go. This is when you, the dad-in-waiting, switch from standby to captain, ensuring everything from the hospital bag to the car keys are ready to roll.

Stages of Labor Explained

Labor is like a three-act play; knowing each stage is crucial to your supportive role. The first stage is early labor when the cervix dilates and effaces. It's like watching the pre-game show—it can be long, sometimes exciting, and often just a waiting game. This could take hours or even days, so there's no point in pacing around like a nervous wreck trying to speed things up.

The second stage is the main event when active labor begins. The cervix is fully dilated, and it's time for your partner to push. Think of it as the climax of a marathon. The finish line is in sight, the crowd (in this case, the medical team) is cheering, and you're there to provide the isotonic drinks (or, in this case, encouragement and support).

The third stage is the delivery of the placenta, also called the afterbirth. It's less intense but still significant. It's like the cool-down after an intense workout, necessary to complete the process.

9.2 ESSENTIAL SUPPORT ROLES DURING DELIVERY

Imagine being a wingman on the biggest mission of your life. Your job is to ensure the star pilot, your partner, has everything she needs to get through the intense and amazing childbirth experience. It's not just holding her hand; it's about being her advocate, her physical support, and her emotional rock, all while capturing these moments and not missing a thing.

Advocacy for Your Partner

Being there for your partner during delivery is like being her representative in a major negotiation. You are there to express her wishes and concerns, ensuring that her wishes are front and center. This means you need to have a deep understanding of the birth plan. Does she want to avoid certain procedures? What does she think about pain management? These are important things to know. You are like her spokesperson at a press conference; every word you communicate affects how her delivery story is told. Engage actively with the medical team, ask questions, and relay information to her, ensuring she feels heard and respected. It's about ensuring the medical staff sees her as a person, not just another patient. If things start moving quickly and decisions must be made, your role as her advocate is vital. You'll need to balance sensitivity with assertiveness—ensuring her voice isn't lost in the whirlwind of labor.

Physical Support Techniques

Now, let's talk about physical support. Because, let's be real, labor is a marathon, and every athlete needs a good physio. From mastering the art of the lower back massage to understanding the mechanics of supportive positioning, your hands are more powerful than you think. Start with simple massage techniques to help alleviate her pain during contractions. Applying gentle pressure to her lower back or rubbing her shoulders can do wonders. Be ready to help her into different positions, whether she needs to walk around to ease the pain or lean on you during contractions. Not only does this help her manage her pain, but it also helps to deepen your connection, showing her that you are there for her every step of the way.

Emotional Reassurance

Emotional support is a big deal. It can affect how your partner experiences labor. You've got to do more than say, "You can do this." You have to show her you believe it. Look her in the eye, use affirmative language, and don't waver in your confidence in her strength. If she starts to panic, remind her of her power and the milestones you've already crossed together. Sometimes, all she needs is for you to be there, holding her hand, breathing with her.

Documenting the Moment

In the age of smartphones, everyone's a photographer, but during delivery, your role needs to balance documentation with participation. Establish beforehand how much she's comfortable with you recording. Some moments might be for your eyes only, while others can be captured to share with the world. Remember to be respectful and present, whether snapping a quick photo of her gripping your hand, recording the first cry, or capturing the quiet intensity of her focus. These snippets of time are priceless, capturing the raw, natural essence of the birth experience. But never let the lens interfere with your primary role as her support. Stay mindful of the balance—her needs should dictate your actions, not the perfect camera angle.

In the whirlwind of delivery, you have many roles, each crucial. You need to speak up for her with the medical staff, help her physically, and keep the mood positive. And remember, as much as physical support is important, emotional support is invaluable. Just focus on what she needs, be flexible, and be there for her. Keep your focus on her needs, stay flexible, and let your steady support be the backbone of her delivery experience. Keep these tips in your back pocket, ready to deploy as you step into the delivery room, where you both will meet your newest family member for the first time.

9.3 UNDERSTANDING DIFFERENT BIRTHING SCENARIOS AND INTERVENTIONS

Not all the plays in the parenting playbook are simple, and the same goes for the birthing process. Think of it as a game day where the coach (that's you) has to adapt to different plays depending on how the game (labor) goes. You have your standard plays like natural birth, where it's just your partner, her body, and a lot of breathing exercises. This is the old-school, ground-and-pound kind of play. It's about as straightforward as it gets, often in a calm environment, perhaps some mood music, and emphasizing minimal medical intervention.

Then there's the assisted birth scenario. This is more like calling in the special teams when you need extra help to get the job done. Tools like forceps or a vacuum may be used to help deliver the baby in the final stages of labor. Why would these be necessary? If the baby is trying to pull a quarterback sneak and is a little stuck, these tools are like extra linemen that help them get into the endzone.

But there's another option, one that's more like a strategic play you didn't plan to call but might need to— the C-section. This is major surgery, and it's reserved for when natural or assisted deliveries aren't safe or possible. Consider it the medical equivalent of switching to a pass-heavy attack when the running game isn't cutting it. Whether it's because the baby is breech or labor isn't progressing as it should, this procedure involves delivering the baby through incisions in the abdomen and uterus. It's more common than you might think, and hey, it gets the team to the end zone safely.

Water birth is where it gets interesting—it's like deciding to play in the rain because it might give your team the edge. In this scenario, your partner is submerged in a warm water birthing pool, which can help ease labor pain and smooth delivery. It's not for everyone, but it's a game-changer for some.

As for the standard interventions, you have inductions and epidurals. Induction is when you start the game early because the weather forecast says a storm is coming. It's used to start labor through medications or other means if things aren't progressing naturally.

An epidural is all about pain management—it's like the defensive line providing a solid block, giving your partner relief from the intensity of the contractions. As for episiotomies, think of them as a last-minute audible at the line of scrimmage—sometimes, a small cut is made to enlarge the opening for the baby to come out more easily.

And emergencies? Yes, those can happen as well. Sometimes, things happen that you didn't expect, such as prolapsed cords or sudden changes in the baby's heartbeat. Here, it's all about quick thinking and trusting your medical team to make the right decisions.

Post-birth, there are a few standard procedures you'll see. Cutting the umbilical cord can be your job if you're up for it—think of it as doing the honors of spiking the ball after a touchdown. Then, there's the magic of skin-to-skin contact, which is crucial for bonding and beneficial for both mom and baby's health. Lastly, the medical team will do a quick but thorough check-up on your rookie player to ensure everything's A-OK.

Navigating these various scenarios might sound daunting, but remember, you're not just a spectator here; you're part of the team. Each decision and support you provide is about making the birthing experience as safe and positive as possible. So put on your game face, keep this playbook handy, and get ready to support your MVP through the biggest game of her life.

Remember that every birth is different, and you are there to adjust and support as necessary. Whether that means cheering on a natural birth, helping with an epidural, or being there for a C-section, you are needed. As we finish this chapter and move on to the next, remember that the main goal is a safe birth and a healthy baby. Get ready because the big day is coming, and you're about to meet your new little buddy.

9.4 BONDING WITH YOUR BABY: THE FIRST TOUCH

Think of the first hours with your newborn as the ultimate meet-and-greet event. Only, instead of awkward handshakes and forgettable small talk, you're diving straight into the deep end of emotional connections and life-altering experiences. It's less about exchanging business cards and more about swapping lifelong commitments. Here's your step-by-step guide to making the most of these first unforgettable moments.

Your baby has just made their grand entrance, and there's this golden hour—a magical window of opportunity that's pure Hollywood script material. The first hour after birth is when your baby is most alert and ready to bond. This isn't just feel-good fluff; it's science-backed magic. Skin-to-skin contact during this time can kickstart everything from better breastfeeding outcomes to regulating the baby's body temperature and heart rate. Imagine lying there, your newborn on your chest, as both heartbeats synchronize in a silent symphony. It's like the ultimate team-building exercise where the team is just you and your new buddy, figuring out the ropes of this new relationship. This moment isn't just beneficial; it's essential, setting the tone for your ongoing father-child bonding.

Your activities during these early hours can set the stage for a lifelong bond. Simple interactions like gentle stroking, eye contact, or softly talking to your baby can have profound effects. These actions signal to your baby that you're more than just a bystander. You're a key player in their world. It's like putting down the first layer of bricks in your relationship. Every little interaction and every touch is a brick in this foundation, building a solid base of love and trust.

CHAPTER 10
BABY BASICS:
A DAD'S GUIDE TO NEWBORNS

Think of the first time you tried to change a tire—tools laid out, manual in one hand, phone in the other with a how-to video queued up. Now, replace the tire with a wiggly baby and the tools with diapers and wipes. Welcome to the pit stop of fatherhood, where speed and efficiency meet safety and care. This is Diaper Changing 101, the class you never knew you needed but one you'll want to ace for the sanity of your baby and nostrils.

10.1 DIAPER CHANGING 101: TIPS AND TRICKS

Navigating the Aisles of Absorbency

First things first, let's talk hardware—diapers. Walking into the diaper aisle can be like trying to choose a cereal in the supermarket; the options seem endless, yet all the same. You have basic disposable diapers, eco-friendly alternatives, and cloth varieties. Each has its fans and uses, like choosing between a sports car, a sedan, or a rugged SUV.

Disposables are your best bet if you want something fast—easy to use, absorbent, and you can throw them away. But if you're environmentally conscious or looking to save money, cloth diapers are the way to go. They require more work at first, but they are like reusable grocery bags for your baby's bum. And then there are the hybrids, which use a cloth cover and a disposable insert, giving you the best of both worlds. Your choice depends on your life, your baby's likes, and how much you hate laundry.

Setting Up Your Pit Stop

Now, let's talk about setting up your diaper-changing station. Think of it like setting up a small workshop. You should have all the essentials: diapers, baby wipes, a water bottle (for drinking and emergency cleanups), diaper rash cream, and a toy. Having a small toy is a necessity for a squirmy infant. Lay everything out within arm's reach, and if you're using a changing table, consider a comfortable mat for the baby—soft but easy to wipe clean. Never leave your baby unattended on a high surface, not even for a second. It's like taking your eyes off a boiling pot; it may be okay nine times out of ten, but that tenth time will cause a mess.

The Art of the Change

Let's face it: diaper duty can seem like a nightmare, but don't worry, we've got you covered. Check out this incredibly helpful instructional video by Jason Kreidman from Dad University. He'll show you step-by-step how to tackle this task like a seasoned pro. Watch the video at http://www.youtube.com/watch?v=CAPjF-RCpro&t=321s, or scan the QR code below and get ready to transform diaper duty from daunting to doable!

It might take a few extra steps with snaps or inserts for cloth diapers, but the concept is the same. Ensure there are no gaps and the diaper is not too tight or rubbing the skin. Eventually, you'll get to the point where you can change a diaper as fast as a NASCAR pit stop.

Dealing with Curveballs

No matter how good you are, you'll eventually encounter a hiccup. A squirmy baby can turn a simple diaper change into an all-out wrestling match. The trick is to distract them and work fast. Give them a toy or make silly faces to keep them from thinking about what you're doing. For diaper changes at night, try to keep things calm. Use a low light and speak softly to help your baby get back to sleep after the change.

Night-time changes are like negotiating with a sleepless diplomat. You want to be quick, efficient, and as unobtrusive as possible. You should keep diapers and wipes within easy reach of the crib so you can get in and out as quickly as possible. And remember, it's all a learning process. You'll get better at it with time.

FYI, Changing a baby boy's diaper can be like a game of Russian roulette. The instant the diaper comes off, you could be in for a surprise geyser. One late-night diaper change, I was feeling pretty confident. I had wipes and a fresh diaper ready to go when my little guy decided to turn it into a fountain. Like the rookie dad I was, I tried to shield myself from the spray with my hands. It went everywhere—on the walls, the floor, and, of course, all over me. I quickly learned to place a cloth or baby wipe over the area to minimize the mess. Pro tip: keep an extra shirt nearby for those unexpected showers.

10.2 UNDERSTANDING NEWBORN SLEEP PATTERNS

Imagine a world where night and day blur together, like a 24-hour diner that never closes. That's what it's like with a newborn. And it's about more than just getting used to staying awake at all hours of the night. It's also about understanding the differences between your sleep patterns and your baby's. Unlike adults, who go through periods of deep and light sleep, newborns spend most of their time in what is known as active sleep. This is similar to the adult REM (Rapid Eye Movement) stage, where dreams happen. Sleep is lighter and more easily disturbed for your baby, leading to frequent wake-ups that can test the patience of even the most saintly new fathers.

Setting realistic expectations comes down to accepting that, at first, your baby will wake up about every two to three hours to eat, which is normal at this stage. They have small stomachs and must eat often to keep up with their rapid growth. It's like having a little car with a small gas tank. It's not a mistake in the design; it's just how it is with babies.

Your next step is to create a sleep-friendly environment. That doesn't mean you have to deck out the nursery with blackout curtains and soundproof walls, although those can be helpful. It's more about creating a space that promotes comfort and safety, allowing your baby to fall asleep more easily. Begin by setting the room temperature to around 68 to 72 degrees. That way, your baby will be at an ambient temperature and won't overheat or get too cold, which can disrupt sleep.

Noise levels are important, too. While you might think a quiet room is best, remember that your baby has just spent nine months in the womb, where the sounds of your partner's heartbeat and whoosh of blood were constant. A white noise machine can replicate these sounds and help block out other distracting noises. Keep it at a safe distance from the crib, and turn it on every night when you put your baby to bed.

A consistent bedtime routine can be a big help. This isn't about strict schedules or keeping track of the time to the minute. It's about reminding your baby that it's time to get ready for bed. This could be something as simple as a warm bath, a quiet song, and a feeding. Each part of the routine is like a little push towards sleep, helping to maintain a sleep pattern despite their growing senses.

Navigating sleep challenges is where you'll really be tested. Night wakings are a common issue that leaves many parents at a loss. But instead of worrying about every time your baby wakes up, use these moments to reinforce your training. A soft pat, a gentle shush, or even letting your baby find their way back to sleep can all help teach them to soothe themselves. As for sleep regressions, when great sleepers suddenly decide they want to be awake all night, remember that these are just phases. Growth spurts or developmental leaps often cause them and don't last forever. Don't hesitate to talk to your pediatrician if you're struggling or the problem persists. Sometimes, a professional opinion can give you strategies or simply reassure you that what you're experiencing is normal.

Mastering these elements—decoding sleep cycles, crafting a nurturing environment, establishing routines, and tackling sleep challenges—will help your baby get better rest. You'll also set the stage for healthier sleep habits that can benefit the entire family, making those dreamy nights more of a reality.

10.3 SOOTHING TECHNIQUES AND HANDLING A FUSSY BABY

Imagine it's the fourth quarter, your team is down by one, the crowd is roaring, and you've got the ball. The pressure's intense, and you need a strategy that's guaranteed to work. Now, replace the ball with your fussy newborn, and instead of scoring a touchdown, your goal is to bring peace and calm to your little one (Please don't spike the baby). Soothing a fussy baby is like being the clutch player everyone's counting on, and I've got the play-by-play to help you nail it every time.

The Art of Baby Burrito Making

First, let's talk swaddling, an age-old technique that's essentially baby burrito making. In this technique, you wrap your baby tightly in a blanket, mimicking the womb. But this isn't just about comfort; it's about creating a sense of security that calms the baby's startle reflex. Check out this informative video on swaddling by The Doctors Bjorkman at http://www.youtube.com/watch?v=ayjlY3RnTrE&t=580s. You can also scan the QR code below.

The Sound of Calm

Next, let's talk about how to use white noise and shushing to soothe your baby. Remember, your baby has spent months in a constant white noise machine—the womb. This environment is surprisingly loud, and your baby may find it very calming to hear similar sounds.

White noise is a consistent sound that helps to mask other sounds. You can use a fan, an air conditioner, or even a white noise machine to create the sound. The key is that it should be consistent and quiet enough. Think of a gentle rain, not a hurricane.

Shushing is also a great way to soothe your baby, but it's not just about being quiet. Shushing is an active soothing technique in which you make a strong, steady "shush" sound near your baby's ear. It's similar to the sound they heard in the womb and can effectively transform cries into yawns.

Rock-a-Bye Baby

Movement is another incredibly effective soothing technique. Rocking is one of the most effective ways of calming a baby. Whether you sit in a rocking chair, sway back and forth, or walk with your baby snug in a carrier, rocking is a reminder of the rocking they felt in the womb.

If you opt for a baby swing, ensure it's used responsibly. Swings are great for providing that consistent motion that babies crave. But they're no substitute for human touch and should always be used under supervision. Think of the swing as the relief pitcher in baseball—they're great for a couple of innings but won't play the whole game.

The Natural Soothing Technique

Lastly, let's not forget about pacifiers and sucking. Sucking is a natural self-soothing mechanism. Whether it's a pacifier, thumb, or finger, sucking helps calm the baby's nervous system and reduces crying. Using a pacifier can be a great way to give your baby a way to soothe themselves without always needing to eat.

However, like any great sports strategy, timing is everything. It's usually best to introduce a pacifier after breastfeeding has been well established to avoid any confusion that could disrupt feeding. When picking out a pacifier, consider the size and material—silicone is durable and easy to clean, and the size should be suitable for your baby's age to ensure safety and effectiveness.

Mastering these soothing techniques—swaddling, white noise, movement, and sucking—is about more than just calming your baby. It's about enhancing your connection, building trust, and becoming the MVP in your baby's eyes. Each technique, each gentle sway, and each soothing shush is a step towards a deeper bond. So equip yourself with these strategies, and you'll be ready to turn those cries into contented coos, proving once again that you've got the magic touch when it comes to being a dad.

10.4 SPLISH SPLASH: THE BASICS OF BABY BATHING

Imagine it's your first time piloting a submarine. The bathroom is steamy, the sound of water fills the air, and you must successfully navigate this maiden voyage without flooding the engine. I.e., you need to keep the baby happy and keep the water at just the right temperature. Welcome to the captain's chair of baby bathing, where you will soon learn that the right mix of warmth, soap, and songs can turn a splash session into an enjoyable bonding experience.

Timing Those First Splashes

First things first, when do you start bathing your baby? Despite what you might think, it's not right away. In fact, you should wait until the umbilical cord stump falls off and heals, which usually takes one to four weeks. Why? Because immersing that area in water could introduce bacteria and lead to infection. Until then, a sponge bath will do. It's like a warm-up for the real thing, getting your baby used to the water but not submerged. During this time, you should keep the face, neck, and diaper area clean, using a damp washcloth to gently wipe and keep these areas fresh.

Setting the Stage for a Splashtastic Time

Now, let's get ready for those full-on baby baths. This is more of a tactical operation than just a splash in the water. First, you'll need a baby tub or a sink insert, some mild baby soap, two washcloths (one for the face and one for the bum), a soft towel, and a clean diaper and clothes for afterward. The water temperature is key. You want it to be lukewarm, around 98.6°F, or what feels comfortable to the inside of your wrist, not just your hand. Too hot or too cold, and you'll have a fight on your hands from the get-go.

Make it a calm place. You don't have to hurry; it's more like preparing a spa day for your kid. A warm room, no cold air, some soft music, and maybe even a couple of rubber ducks could make bath time a pleasant experience instead of a rush. Make sure everything is close at hand so you don't have to reach or, worse, leave the room. And always make sure it's safe.

After Bath Care

Once you're done bathing, wrap your baby in a soft, warm towel and pat them dry, being careful around the umbilical area. Apply a hypoallergenic, fragrance-free moisturizer to prevent dry skin, and get them dressed quickly to keep them warm. You can also give them some extra cuddles while you dry them off to keep them warm after the bath.

Remember, bathing your baby is more than just getting them clean. It's a way to bond, build trust, and set the stage for unforgettable father-child moments. In these moments, while the water is running and your baby is splashing around, you are not just cleaning up but stepping up as a father.

10.5 BOTTLE FEEDING BASICS FOR DADS

Imagine stepping into the role of a seasoned bartender, except your customer is under two feet tall and has a very limited palate. This is the world of bottle feeding, where precision meets patience and every ounce counts. Let's break down the essentials, from picking the proper hardware to ensuring each feeding session is as smooth as a well-aged whiskey, minus the alcohol.

The Dad's Guide to Liquid Gold

First, selecting the right bottle and formula is akin to choosing the right golf club—it can make or break your game. Bottles come in various sizes, shapes, and materials, each with unique benefits. You've got anti-colic bottles with special vents to keep air bubbles out of your baby's dinner, angled bottles designed to reduce gas and ear infections, and the straightforward classic bottle that's been around since your dad was in diapers. Material-wise, there's plastic, which is lightweight and practically indestructible; glass, which is easy to clean and free from chemicals but handles like a live grenade; and stainless steel, which is durable and insulates well but comes with a heftier price tag.

When it comes to formula, if your baby's tummy is the barometer, then you're the weatherman, predicting which way the wind will blow. Will it be a smooth day with a basic milk-based formula, or are storm clouds of gas and fussiness on the horizon signaling a need for a sensitive or hypoallergenic formula? For babies with allergies or intolerance, the formula aisle offers everything from soy-based to lactose-free and everything in between, ensuring you can find the mix that works best for your little connoisseur.

The Art of Bottle Feeding

Next, let's talk about the technique. Bottle feeding is not just about sticking a bottle in your baby's mouth and hoping for the best. There's a right way to do it: the right hold, angle, and pace. Start with the "cuddle hold," where your baby's head rests in the crook of your elbow, which not only encourages bonding and eye contact but also allows you to monitor the tilt of the bottle. The bottle should be tilted so the nipple is filled with milk and no air can sneak in.

Pacing is crucial. It's not a race to the finish line; it's more about enjoying the journey. Keep the pace slow and easy; let the baby set the pace. Look for signs of eating, like sucking and swallowing, and stop every few minutes to burp the baby. This will help with air intake and reduce the amount of discomfort afterward so that the burps are more like puffs of air rather than full-on belches.

Cleaning and Sterilization

Post-feeding, think of yourself as the cleanup crew after a big party. You've got to wash every bottle, nipple, and cap to keep your little guy or gal safe:

1. Rinse everything in cold water.
2. Use hot, soapy water and a bottle brush to clean the inside of the nipples and bottles, making sure to get all the milk.
3. You can sterilize them by boiling them for five minutes, using an electric steam sterilizer, or putting them in the microwave.

Each method has its merits, but all aim to keep your baby's feeding tools pristine and free from bacteria and other unwelcome germs.

The Dad's Role in Feeding Harmony

If your baby's dining options include breast and bottle, consider yourself the maître d' of a fine dining establishment, where coordination is key to a seamless experience. The goal is to support breastfeeding and bottle feeding without causing preference confusion for your baby. Introducing a bottle only after breastfeeding is well-established, usually taking about three to four weeks. Choose a slow-flow nipple to mimic the effort required during breastfeeding. Encourage your partner to express breast milk for bottle feeding. This not only maintains the nutrient-rich benefits of breast milk but also keeps the flavor consistent, reducing bottle rejection because, let's face it, babies have a palate more discerning than a seasoned food critic.

Regarding both, your job is to ensure your baby can switch between breast and bottle without a hitch. Suppose you pay attention to your baby's signals and are there to feed them when they're hungry. In that case, you'll create a flexible feeding schedule that helps your partner and your baby and even allows you to bond over those late-night feedings. So grab a bottle (the baby's, not yours), and let's make this feeding process as smooth as possible.

10.6 SUPPORTING BREASTFEEDING: A DAD'S ROLE

Breastfeeding might look like a mom-exclusive club, but don't hang your jersey up yet, Dad. Your role in this team effort is more pivotal than you might think. Imagine you're the assistant coach whose strategies and support can make all the difference in a successful season.

Understanding Breastfeeding Basics

Breastfeeding is more than just food; it's a complicated mix of biology, emotion, and physics. It begins with the let-down reflex, where the baby's sucking stimulates nerves in the breast to release milk through tiny ducts. And the benefits are huge. For the baby, breast milk is like a custom mixture of all the nutrients they need, and it even contains antibodies to help protect against disease. For the mother, it can help speed up recovery after childbirth and reduce the risk of certain diseases. Knowing this can help you understand what goes into it, better understand the commitment involved, and help you be a supportive partner rather than a bystander.

Emotional and Physical Support

Your job is to make sure your partner is comfortable when she is feeding. This could be as simple as getting her a glass of water or making sure she has enough pillows to support her back. They might be little things in the big picture, but they keep the machine running. Emotional support is also significant. Breastfeeding can be a difficult time, and your job is to be there to support her. Tell her she's doing great, celebrate the small victories, and listen. Sometimes, that's all she needs.

Troubleshooting Common Issues

Breastfeeding might seem as natural as breathing, but it often comes with challenges. Issues like sore nipples, engorgement, and latching difficulties are common. Recognize these early. If your partner is expressing discomfort beyond typical initial tenderness, it's time to consult a lactation expert. Consider calling in a specialist when the regular playbook isn't cutting it. These pros can help you with hands-on advice and techniques, sometimes solving what seems like a game-ending problem with just a few simple adjustments.

Sharing the Night Shift

Night feedings are part of having a newborn. They can be tiring, but they're not so bad if you share the responsibility. Take over changing diapers and calming the baby after feeding. If your spouse is pumping, you can take a feeding with a bottle to allow her to get some sleep. Think of it as taking turns: one of you sleeps, the other stays up, so you can be more effective.

As you navigate this chapter of early parenthood, remember that your involvement in the breastfeeding process is invaluable. It's about providing support that enhances your partner's experience and contributes positively to your baby's development. Each supportive action, no matter how small, builds a foundation of teamwork and mutual respect that strengthens your family unit.

CHAPTER 11
LITTLE LEAPS

Imagine you've just built a high-tech device with a 'grow-with-you' feature. Sounds cool, right? Well, that's your baby in the first year! From a tiny, sleeping bundle of joy to a wide-eyed explorer. This device, I mean, your baby, doesn't just come with a manual; it writes a new one every few weeks. So, get ready, Dad, because the first three months will be less about fixing problems and more about watching in awe at the rapid updates your baby naturally downloads.

11.1 THE FIRST 3 MONTHS: WHAT TO EXPECT

More Than Meets the Eye

In your baby's first three months, you'll see more growth and development than a tech startup in Silicon Valley. Your baby will undergo a series of physical and sensory upgrades that roll out in new patches each week. Initially, your baby will primarily sleep and eat, but soon, they begin to track objects with their eyes. This isn't just random eye movement; it's your baby's visual software getting updates, allowing them to start understanding and exploring their environment.

Their hearing will also improve. The initially muffled sounds will start to clear up, and they'll turn their heads or startle at sudden noises. It's like watching someone adjust the dial on a radio. Every new sound or sight helps them better understand the world around them. Every new touch they feel, and every shadow they see are part of their sensory exploration app recording data.

Smiles and Social Logins

Get ready for the heart-melting moments when your baby first smiles intentionally. It's not just a wind-induced reflex anymore; this smile is your baby's first attempt at social interaction. These smiles are like the first successful logins into their social world at about six to eight weeks. They start to coo and make other sounds that are not just cute and delightful but are laying the groundwork for future conversations. They're testing their vocal cords, seeing what feels good and what gets a smile in return.

Babies are beginning to recognize faces. If you've ever seen a baby relax at the sight of you, that's the equivalent of clicking "remember me" on a device. They're recognizing their favorite faces and committing those to memory.

Tummy Time Trials

Now, let's talk about motor skills. And I'm not just talking about crawling or walking, but also the ability to hold up their head and control their upper body. It all starts with "tummy time." This is like your baby's daily workout. Just a few minutes a day on their tummy can help strengthen their neck and shoulder muscles so they're ready for the next steps, like sitting up and crawling. Think of it as their basic training for the big leagues of mobility.

System Updates and Reboots

Feeding and sleep are like your baby's necessary system updates and reboots. Whether breastmilk or formula, food is like the high-grade fuel that powers all their growth and system updates. And sleep? That's the crucial downtime when their little bodies reboot and apply all these updates. Setting up a feeding and sleep schedule is like configuring the settings to optimize performance. It won't always be perfect—there will be nights that feel more like system crashes—but gradually, a pattern emerges that lets both baby and parents have a good night's rest.

11.2 4-6 MONTHS: ENCOURAGING GROWTH THROUGH PLAY

As your rookie season of fatherhood progresses, you're about to hit what many coaches in the baby league might call the 'fun phase.' Now, from four to six months, your baby isn't just watching the world you've shown them; they're ready to get involved. This is when play isn't just play; it's a critical learning period where every interaction is a chance to promote growth in every area: physically, cognitively, and emotionally.

Think of playtime now as a series of fun, exploratory experiments. It's about introducing your baby to various textures, sounds, and colors. Let's say you have a play mat set up with toys of different textures—some smooth, some ridged, and others fluffy. Each one of those toys invites your baby to learn and engage differently. As they reach out, grab, and feel each one, they're not just playing but learning about the world around them. The crinkle of a fabric book or the soft jingle of a rattle are more than just noises; they're like the sounds of new characters in a story, each piquing your baby's interest in the world.

You'll see your child reach some significant milestones during these months. First, there's the rolling over. One day, you'll set your baby down on their back; the next thing you know, they've rolled onto their stomach. Then there's the babbling. At first, it's just a bunch of vowels, but then consonants appear. It's not just random noise; think of it as practice for when they're old enough to talk to you about everything from cookies to cartoons.

Next, it's time to start feeding them real food. This isn't just about getting something in their stomachs but about getting them used to the flavors of the family table. Start with single-ingredient foods, which is like giving them the basic building blocks of taste. Each new food is a splash of color on their palate's blank canvas, and your role is to introduce these in a way that turns mealtime into a fun exploration, not a forced march.

Creating a stimulating environment for all this growth is like building the perfect playground. It's not just about putting on the safety locks and padding the corners; it's about making spaces that encourage exploration and interaction. Use baby mirrors for self-discovery, use areas with different colors for visual stimulation, and ensure enough space to move around. Everything in their environment is a teaching tool.

It's also important to help your baby learn how to engage with others. The more your baby interacts with family and friends, the better they will understand social cues and how to form relationships. This could be as easy as getting an older sibling to play peek-a-boo or having the whole family sing a song together. These interactions will help your baby learn about communication, expression, and love.

CHAPTER 12
BABY BLUES AND DADDY DO'S:
A GUIDE FOR POSTPARTUM CARE

Imagine you've just bought a new gadget. It's got buttons, lights, and maybe a few switches that you, frankly, have no clue about. You're excited but slightly nervous because the thing didn't come with a manual. That's sort of what diving into postpartum life is like. You're thrilled about this new phase, but it's packed with complexities that no one prepped you for, especially when it comes to navigating postpartum depression (PPD).

12.1 RECOGNIZING SIGNS OF POSTPARTUM DEPRESSION

Awareness of Symptoms

Postpartum depression isn't just a bad day or a bit of fatigue that your partner can sleep off. It's the heavy, persistent cloud that can affect their entire experience of motherhood and, by extension, your journey into parenthood. Think of PPD as a glitch in the system that needs specific attention, not just a reboot. Symptoms might include:

- A deep sadness.
- A disconnection from the baby.
- A numbness to all the things that used to bring joy. It's

like watching your favorite team lose its spark, except this isn't just a game—it's real life, and it's happening to your MVP.

Now, distinguishing these signs from the typical 'baby blues' is crucial. Baby blues are like the minor leagues—fairly common, affecting up to 80% of new mothers and usually resolving within two weeks without intervention. They're characterized by mood swings, sadness, irritability, and feeling overwhelmed, but they're fleeting. PPD, on the other hand, is the major league. It's intense, lasts longer, and can appear anywhere from a few weeks to a year after delivery. Recognizing this difference helps in tackling the issue before it escalates.

Encouraging Professional Help

Encouraging your partner to seek help can be as tricky as convincing a stubborn player to see the physio. The key is in the approach. Start with empathy, understanding that admitting they need help might make them feel vulnerable or inadequate. It's about gently suggesting a consultation, perhaps starting with a regular check-up and easing into a discussion about deeper concerns. Frame it as a team strategy to ensure the whole family's well-being rather than pointing out a weakness. It's not about fixing a problem but fine-tuning the team's dynamics.

Support Networks

Here's where you draft your dream team. Building a robust support network isn't just about having people to share the load; it's about creating a community that uplifts and sustains both of you. This network might include family, friends, doctors, and even parent groups—think of it as your parenting league, each member bringing something unique to the bench. Importantly, include yourself in this network. Acknowledge that you also need support because the coach needs to be in top shape to manage the team effectively.

Self-Care for Both Parents

In the whirlwind of new parenthood, it's easy to sideline your own needs. But remember, self-care isn't selfish; it's like putting on your oxygen mask first to better assist others. For you and your partner, self-care means catching up on sleep, finding a moment for a favorite hobby, or even grabbing a coffee together. It's about preserving your individuality and sanity amidst the chaos of diapers and late-night feeds. When both of you take care of your well-being, you're setting up your family for a win.

Navigating postpartum depression requires patience, understanding, and proactive engagement. It's about recognizing the signs early, supporting each other through the highs and lows, and always keeping communication open. With the right strategies and support, you can manage this challenging phase and come out stronger, ready to tackle the joys and trials of parenting together. Remember, it's not just about making it through the season; it's about thriving as a team.

12.2 PRACTICAL WAYS TO SUPPORT PHYSICAL RECOVERY

Understanding the Physical Recovery Process

Post-birth, the body isn't just bouncing back—it's undergoing a whole series of repairs and adjustments, much like a car after a long, hard race. The physical recovery process includes everything from the shrinking of the uterus back to its original size (imagine trying to deflate one of those giant exercise balls) to the healing of any tears or cuts made during delivery. It's vital to understand what's expected during this period: a certain amount of bleeding is expected, much like the oil that needs changing after a tough drive, and fatigue is as common as a flat battery in a car that's been idling too long.

However, some signs might require a mechanic's, or in this case, a doctor's attention. These include fever, which could indicate an infection, or unusually heavy bleeding, which might signify complications. Knowing these signs helps you act swiftly, ensuring your partner gets the necessary care without delay.

Assistance with Daily Tasks

Think of the postpartum period as one of those team-building retreats where everyone has to pitch in for success. In this scenario, your partner needs you to step up. Taking over more household duties can be a game changer. This means tackling the laundry monster before it turns into a mountain, keeping the fridge and pantry stocked (because no one should have to grocery shop on two hours of sleep) and handling most cooking—or at least becoming best friends with the most reliable takeout joints.

Childcare responsibilities multiply faster than you'd expect. Diaper changes, soothing sessions, and midnight feedings are all part of the playbook now. By sharing these tasks, you give your partner some much-needed rest and bond with your little one. It's a win-win, except for the sleep score, which might temporarily look like a basketball game's final tally.

Emotional Presence

Being present isn't just about physical help; it's about being there emotionally. Postpartum can sometimes feel as chaotic as a stock market trading floor—highs and lows, with emotions running wild. Your role? Be that calm, steady voice that helps center everything. Listen actively, which means putting down your phone, making eye contact, and really hearing what your partner is expressing without rushing to fix things. Validate her feelings by acknowledging that feeling overwhelmed, sad, or angry is okay. It's about letting her know her feelings are understood and supported, not a problem to be solved.

Promoting Physical Health

Encouraging and participating in gentle physical activities can be incredibly beneficial for your partner's recovery. Think of it as being her personal trainer, but one more focused on health than breaking any records. Begin with simple walks, perhaps around the block or to a local park. It's not just about physical health; these small outings can also provide a mental refresh, a chance to breathe fresh air, and a break from the relentless routine of feed-change-sleep.

As weeks pass, consider activities that can be bonding and beneficial for physical well-being. Yoga, for instance, can be an excellent way for your partner to ease back into exercise, and many places offer classes specifically designed for new moms. Swimming is another low-impact option that can feel wonderfully supportive, literally lifting the weight off her shoulders.

Navigating the postpartum period is like handling a delicate, complex piece of machinery. It requires patience, attentiveness, and the willingness to learn and adapt. Your partner's recovery is not just a pathway back to their pre-pregnancy state; it's a journey of healing and adjustment that demands both physical and emotional support. By stepping up and actively participating in this process, you help create a nurturing environment that promotes quicker recovery and a stronger foundation for your growing family. As you move forward, remember that every small effort counts, building a stronger team and a happier home.

12.3 RECOGNIZING AND MANAGING YOUR OWN MENTAL HEALTH AS A NEW FATHER

Let's face it, gents, the arrival of a newborn, while mostly a parade of joy and baby snuggles, can occasionally feel like you're trying to assemble a space shuttle with a toy screwdriver. Just as mothers can experience postpartum depression, we dads are also on the emotional frontline. The narrative often sidelines fathers, painting us as the support crew rather than co-stars of the postpartum saga. However, statistics throw a rather glaring spotlight on the truth: about 10% of new dads wrestle with postpartum depression, and the numbers spike when their partners are also struggling. These aren't just bad days; we're talking about a persistent fog of sadness, a short fuse at minor irritations, and even a disheartening disconnection from the little one who you know, logically, is supposed to be your mini-me.

Addressing this isn't just crucial; it's imperative for your family's harmony and your personal health. Recognizing the signs early can be a game-changer. Whether it's a lingering irritability that's out of character or a weightiness in your chest that makes mornings a drag, these are your cues to seek help. And no, seeking help isn't about admitting defeat. It's more like tagging in a teammate when you know you're not at your best.

Building a robust support network can feel a bit like trying to schedule a drink with friends—complicated but worth it. Connecting with fellow dads facing similar challenges in this digital age can offer you a lifeline. Whether through online forums, social media groups, or local meet-ups, these connections can act as your sounding board and crisis management team. Sharing experiences and solutions not only eases your sense of isolation but can also equip you with strategies to tackle your challenges more effectively.

Balancing the herculean tasks of fatherhood with personal downtime might sound like a myth, but it's a balance worth striving for. Carving out time for your hobbies, hitting the gym, or simply catching up on sleep are not selfish acts; they recharge your batteries, making you more present and engaged when on daddy duty. Consider this: a well-oiled machine can run longer and more efficiently, and taking care of yourself ensures you're at your best for your little one.

Let's talk shop about communication with your partner. Open dialogues about how you're handling the new dynamics can prevent misunderstandings and foster mutual support. Setting aside time to discuss each other's day or feelings can strengthen your relationship, ensuring you both feel valued and understood. It's not just about co-parenting; it's about maintaining the partnership that forms the foundation of your new family.

Navigating fatherhood, especially in the early stages, is akin to learning a new sport where the rules constantly change. It's dynamic, it's demanding, and yes, it can be daunting. But with the right tools—awareness, support, self-care, and communication—you can manage and thrive during this transformative phase. As we wrap up this chapter, remember that taking care of your mental health is not just a personal priority but a cornerstone of your family's well-being. Each step you take towards recognizing and managing your mental health is a step towards a more fulfilled and joyful fatherhood.

CHAPTER 13
SHOTS AND TOTS:
BABY'S HEALTH JOURNEY

Imagine you're getting ready for the most important game of your life, and the coach hands you a playbook in a language you barely understand. That's what it's like to start learning about vaccinations for your kid. It's confusing and important, and you need to figure it out quickly. This chapter isn't just about giving you the condensed version; it's about making you an expert on the game. So, buckle up as we tackle the big V—vaccinations!

13.1 NAVIGATING VACCINATION DECISIONS

Understanding Vaccination Benefits and Risks

Regarding vaccinations, think of them as your baby's bodyguards. They're like the Secret Service, trained to defend against potential threats. Vaccines introduce a tiny, safe part of a virus or bacteria to your baby's immune system. This is like showing a wanted poster to the sheriff in an old Western movie. It allows your baby's immune system to recognize the bad guys and develop defenses against them without causing the disease.

Like anything else, vaccines have their pros and cons. Most side effects are mild, like a fever or a sore arm. However, severe side effects can and do happen, like with any medical procedure. The key is to weigh the benefits against the risks. The benefits of protecting your child from diseases like measles, whooping cough, and polio far outweigh the risks of a severe reaction. But then, you should always know what you're getting into before you dive in head first.

Communicating with Healthcare Providers

Talking to your pediatrician about vaccines can feel like talking to tech support when you don't understand computers. You need to go in with your game face on, ready to ask the right questions. What vaccines does my child need, and when? What are the risks and benefits?

Keep this dialogue open and respectful. Doctors are like the experienced coaches who have seen it all. They can give you the playbook (or, in this case, the vaccination schedule), explain the game plan, and help you make informed decisions. And remember, there's no such thing as a dumb question regarding your child's health. Each question you ask makes your team stronger, ensuring your little MVP gets the best defense possible.

Exploring Alternative Perspectives

In this day and age, you'll encounter a spectrum of opinions on vaccinations. Some parents delay or even skip vaccinations altogether for various reasons. It's important to listen and understand the various viewpoints. Think of it as scouting the competition. Why do they play the way they do? What strategies are they using?

Understanding different perspectives will help you make your own decisions and respect the choices of others. It doesn't mean you have to agree, but in the end, it's better for everyone if there is no judgment or condemnation in parenting.

Making an Informed Choice

Ultimately, deciding whether to vaccinate your child is like being the quarterback in a critical game. The decision impacts not just your little one but the whole team—your family and, by extension, the wider community. Weighing the benefits of vaccination against potential risks involves understanding the broader implications, like herd immunity, which protects those who can't be vaccinated, such as newborns or those with certain medical conditions.

As you make these decisions, get your information from reliable sources—your doctors, reputable health organizations, and studies that other experts have reviewed. Don't get distracted by the false information on the internet and from other people's experiences. It's about making a move based on what you know will work and what's best for your child.

13.2 VACCINATION SCHEDULE AND HEALTH CHECK-UPS

Keeping track of when to vaccinate your child is like keeping track of your favorite team's games. You have to know when to show up and what's at stake. It's important to stay on track with your child's vaccinations to protect them from all the germs out there. Think of each vaccination as an important game; your child's health is on the line. If you miss a game, you miss protection from diseases like measles, mumps, and whooping cough. Each shot is given at a specific time in your child's development to offer the best protection when they need it most.

These appointments aren't just a quick in and out for a shot; they're a complete look at how your baby grows. Think of them as your baby's regular season check-ups, where you ensure they are still growing in weight, length, and head circumference, much like a coach checks up on his players to ensure they are still in shape. This is important as it can give you an early indication of your baby's overall health and catch any potential problems early.

During these check-ups, your pediatrician will also do developmental screenings, which are tests to see if your baby is on track with things like rolling over, crawling, paying attention, learning, communicating, and socializing. These things are important for a baby's development, and catching any potential problems early can make a big difference.

Now, when it comes to anticipating problems, you come in as the advocate and the coach. You need to speak up during these visits if you notice anything strange about your child's development or something that seems off. Perhaps your six-month-old isn't making eye contact like they should, or your nine-month-old isn't babbling like the other babies. You need to bring these things up. After all, you're the one who spends all day with your baby, and if you can spot these things early on, it gives your doctor a head start.

Every play counts in this game of growing up, and ensuring you are on top of the health game will keep your baby healthy and growing strong. Keep this conversation going so you are not just listening to what you're told but also involved in your child's health. This is a great way to keep your baby healthy, growing, and ready to take on the world.

13.3 HOME SAFETY FOR CRAWLERS AND WALKERS

When your little adventurer starts to crawl or walk, your home is suddenly a playground with lots of fun things to do and many ways to get hurt. You have to start seeing your house from the point of view of a little one with a mission to touch, taste, and knock over everything in sight. Baby-proofing isn't just about putting bumpers on sharp corners; it's about making sure your baby can explore safely and keep the crying (and the injuries) to a minimum.

Think of baby-proofing as prepping the playing field. Start with the basics: electrical outlets are like magnets for tiny fingers, so get those outlet covers on faster than you can say "No!". Next, secure heavy furniture and TVs to the walls—these can tip over with surprising ease when used as a baby's support for standing up. Don't forget the small objects and choking hazards; if it's small enough to fit through a paper towel roll, it's small enough to be a danger. This includes everything from grandma's favorite earrings found on the coffee table to that one lone grape that rolled under the couch last year.

Baby gates are like goalies in the game of home safety, and you need them to block off places like staircases or kitchens. It's best to use gates that screw into the wall, not the pressure-fit kind that a child can push over.

Creating safe play areas is like designing a mini amusement park where the safety measures are as robust as the fun. Choose a specific play area in your home where you can lay down shock-absorbent play mats to cushion falls. Make sure this area is away from high-traffic zones to avoid collisions. Fill it with age-appropriate toys that encourage various physical activities, from crawling under tunnels to stacking blocks. This activity keeps your child engaged and helps develop their motor skills in a controlled environment.

When it comes to keeping little ones safe outdoors, it's the same, just with a few extra items. Whether it's your backyard, a park, or a playground, the first rule is to always keep an eye on them. It only takes a moment for a child to get into trouble. Also, use sun hats and child-safe sunscreen to protect their skin from the sun, and ensure any outdoor play equipment is appropriate for their age and in good condition. Check for loose screws, rusty chains, or cracked plastic that could pose a danger. If you're going a little further, like a hiking trail or beach, have the right equipment, such as a baby carrier for rough terrain and a baby life jacket for water safety.

Finally, no general would go into battle without knowing what to do if his men were injured, and as a parent, neither should you. Learn basic first aid, including CPR and the Heimlich for infants and toddlers. Keep a well-stocked first aid kit in your house and a smaller one in your diaper bag. Know the signs of common accidents like choking, falls, and poisoning, and have emergency numbers, including the local poison control center, saved in your phone and posted in a prominent place at home.

For a crash course in baby first aid, check out this fantastic video by Nicklaus Children's Hospital. They break down the essentials with practical advice. Trust me, it's worth the watch for the peace of mind and potential life you could save. You can find the video at http://www.youtube.com/watch?v=gHZdBY-CkGw&t=2s or scan the QR code below.

SHOTS AND TOTS: 151

CHAPTER 14
ROMANCE AND RATTLES:
BALANCING LOVE AND PARENTING

I magine that your romantic life with your partner is like a favorite TV show you both loved watching together. Then, suddenly, it's as if every episode now features a new main character: your baby. The plot has thickened, and the dynamics have certainly changed. It's easy to feel like your once binge-watchable series might become an occasional clip show. Fear not! This chapter is about turning what could feel like a series finale into an exciting new season premiere, where you learn to balance the roles of doting parents and devoted partners with some panache and a sprinkle of planning.

14.1 KEEPING THE SPARK ALIVE: DATE NIGHTS POST-BABY

Navigating the waters of parenthood doesn't mean letting the ship of romance sail without you. Think of your date nights now as less about grand gestures and more about grabbing those key moments of connection that fuel the relationship. Whether it's a quiet dinner after the baby's bedtime or a full-on date night with babysitters enlisted, it's about quality over quantity.

Creative Date Night Ideas

Let's kick off with some creative date night strategies. Remember, flexibility is your new best friend. Consider at-home date nights where you can enjoy a movie or a candlelit dinner after the baby sleeps. These don't require a babysitter and can be as special as a night out. For the nights when cabin fever hits and you both need a change of scenery, think of low-stress environments that won't make you anxious about being away from the baby. Maybe it's a quiet dinner at your favorite restaurant or a quick coffee date while the baby is with the grandparents. The idea is to create a scenario where you can step out of your parenting roles and into your romantic ones, even if just for an hour or two.

Scheduling Quality Time

Time management is crucial. Sync your calendars to schedule regular date nights or quiet times together. This might sound like corporate-level logistics, but it's about prioritizing your relationship. Treat these moments as important meetings that you can't just reschedule on a whim. Early planning also helps manage expectations and reduces the stress of last-minute scrambles. Whether it's a weekly or bi-weekly slot, having a predictable schedule helps keep the commitment real and the practice regular.

Balancing Parenting and Partnership

Balancing parenting duties with maintaining a romantic relationship with your partner can often feel like trying to solve a Rubik's cube —complex and frustrating if you don't approach it correctly. The key here is to remember that you're partners first. Simple gestures can make a big difference. Something as small as taking over the morning baby routine to let your partner sleep in can feel as grand as sending a dozen roses once did. It's about showing love through support and understanding, reaffirming that your relationship is the foundation on which your family is built.

Involving Family or Sitters

When planning those much-needed escapes, involving family members or trusted babysitters can give you peace of mind. Start by introducing the sitter to your baby well ahead of time, allowing them to become a familiar face, easing your baby's anxiety and yours. If family members are involved, set clear expectations about your baby's routine and needs. It's about building a circle of trust that allows you and your partner to step away briefly without worry.

Keeping the spark alive in your relationship post-baby is about creatively navigating your new reality and making the most of the moments you carve out for each other. It's less about grand gestures and more about meaningful connections, less about quantity of time, and more about quality. By integrating these strategies into your new routine, you ensure that the romantic subplot in your family series remains as compelling as ever, ready to evolve and adapt through the seasons of life.

14.2 COMMUNICATION AND TEAMWORK IN PARENTING

Think of your family as a team where every member plays a crucial role, and good communication is the glue that holds everything together. It's like being on a basketball court where passing the ball effectively can make or break the game. In parenting, maintaining open lines of communication ensures that both you and your partner can pass the ball back and forth without dropping it. This means having regular, honest discussions about everything from who does the night feeds to how you both feel about screen time for your little one. It's about creating a space to speak openly without judgment, ensuring problems are aired before they become full-blown crises.

Consider setting aside a specific time each week for a check-in. This isn't just about logistical planning but also touching base emotionally. How is everyone really feeling? Are the current household rhythms working for both of you? These check-ins can help prevent resentment brewed from unspoken frustrations and ensure that minor issues are discussed before they turn into major grievances. It's akin to holding regular team meetings where strategies are developed and everyone's opinions are valued.

Moving on to blending different parenting styles, it's a bit like mixing cocktails. You might have different ingredients you'd like to add based on your backgrounds, beliefs, and experiences. The key is finding a recipe that suits both tastes without overwhelming one flavor. For instance, if one of you is more about strict routines (think 'Old Fashioned': strong and structured) and the other is more laid-back (more of a 'Mojito': light and flexible), your parenting style might be a perfect blend of both. Discuss these differences openly and find a middle ground that respects both perspectives. This helps create a unified parenting front and respects individual preferences, making the journey smoother and more enjoyable.

Teamwork in decision-making is another critical area. It's about ensuring both voices are heard and valued, from deciding on the baby formula brand to choosing the right preschool. Every decision should be approached with a team mindset. Think of it as a game of doubles tennis – both players need to be in sync, communicate effectively, and play to each other's strengths to win the game. When both partners feel involved in the decision-making process, it leads to better outcomes and strengthens the relationship.

Lastly, acknowledging and appreciating each other cannot be overstated. Parenting, much like any demanding job, can be exhausting and thankless. A simple 'thank you' for handling the bedtime routine or acknowledging how well the other handled a toddler's public meltdown can mean the world. It's about seeing and appreciating the hard work each puts in, which can significantly boost morale. Remember, gratitude is like oil in a well-oiled machine; it keeps everything running smoothly without unnecessary friction.

KEEPING THE GAME ALIVE

Now that you have everything you need to navigate pregnancy, manage delivery room expectations, and master key parenting skills, it's time to pass on your newfound knowledge and show other readers where they can find the same help.

Simply by leaving your honest opinion of this book on Amazon, you'll show other first-time dads where they can find the information they're looking for, and pass their passion for fatherhood forward.

Thank you for your help. The journey of fatherhood is kept alive when we pass on our knowledge – and you're helping me to do just that.

Scan this QR code:

https://www.amazon.com/review/create-review/?asin=B0DKSQCDCP

CONCLUSION

Well, guys, you've made it through the wilderness of fatherhood. Let's take a moment to recap the critical milestones we've navigated together. From the initial shock of finding out you're going to be a dad through the pregnancy and the first months of parenthood. We've covered practical skills such as changing diapers at 3 AM and how to keep the spark alive.

The role of fathers has indeed transformed, and so have the expectations. It's no longer about being a bystander but about being more involved, more emotionally present, and more of a participant. The unique challenges of modern fatherhood, such as balancing work and family life, are now part of your journey. So, embrace it, gentlemen. No more standing on the sidelines. You're now a key player in your family team, and you possess all the necessary tools to take the lead.

As we conclude this chapter (quite literally), remember that being a father is not a destination but a journey of continuous growth. Continue to be a remarkable dad by staying adaptable and always ready to learn—from books, from your partner, from fellow dads, and, yes, most importantly, from your own missteps. Your own experiences are valuable lessons in fatherhood, and while some may be challenging, each one will shape you into a better man and father.

So, here's what you do, guys:

1. Jump into the fray.
2. Pick up that diaper bag and go to the park, the doctor, and even baby yoga with your head held high.
3. Show everyone that today's fathers do more than change diapers.

You're here to change the game.

And one last thing: You've got this. Every single one of you can handle the late nights, the early mornings, the "why" phase, and everything in between. Embrace those challenges and the joys of raising your child. It's not easy; it's the ultimate test of endurance and patience. But let me tell you, when you see that first unsolicited smile or hear that first unprompted "I love you, Dad," you'll know it's all worth it. Fatherhood is the weirdest, scariest, funniest, and most rewarding thing you'll ever do. And remember to keep your sense of humor handy. You're going to need it.

Here's to you, dads. You're doing great.

REFERENCES

- Emerson Hospital. (2021 July 22). *New dads and mental health*. Emerson Hospital. https://www.emersonhospital.org/articles/new-dads-and-mental-health
- NCT. (n.d.). *How to communicate with your partner after having a baby*. NCT. https://www.nct.org.uk/life-parent/your-relationship-couple/relationship-challenges-and-support/how-communicate-your-partner-after-having-baby
- Dad University. (2023 January 20). *New dad anxiety: How to overcome the fear of fatherhood*. Dad University. https://www.daduniversity.com/blog/new-dad-anxiety-how-to-overcome-the-fear-of-fatherhood
- Zen Guided. (2023 July 24). *Meditation for expecting fathers*. Zen Guided. https://zenguided.com/meditation-for-expecting-fathers/
- Gottman Institute. (n.d.). *One conversation new parents need to stay connected*. Gottman Institute. https://www.gottman.com/blog/one-conversation-new-parents-need-stay-connected/
- COPE. (n.d.). *Managing stress as a dad*. COPE. https://www.cope.org.au/family-community/fathers-partners/managing-stress-dad/
- Gottman Institute. (n.d.). *The transition to parenthood: Relationship tips for new parents*. Gottman Institute. https://www.gottman.com/blog/the-transition-to-parenthood-relationship-tips-for-new-parents/
- Postpartum Support International. (n.d.). *Help for dads*. Postpartum Support International. https://www.postpartum.net/get-help/help-for-dads/
- What to Expect. (2022 May 18). *How dads can support their partner during pregnancy*. What to Expect. https://www.whattoexpect.com/pregnancy/dads-guide/support-partner-during-pregnancy/
- Mayo Clinic. (2022 November 04). *First trimester: Your pregnancy week by week*. Mayo Clinic. https://www.mayoclinic.org/healthy-lifestyle/pregnancy-week-by-week/basics/first-trimester/hlv-20049471
- UCSF Health. (n.d.). *Coping with common discomforts of pregnancy*. UCSF Health. https://www.ucsfhealth.org/education/coping-with-common-discomforts-of-pregnancy
- What to Expect. (2022 June 13). *Week-by-week pregnancy advice for dads*

- *and partners*. What to Expect. https://www.whattoexpect.com/pregnancy/for-dad/week-by-week-pregnancy-advice-dads-partners/#first
- What to Expect. (2023 October 05). *Week-by-week pregnancy guide*. What to Expect. https://www.whattoexpect.com/pregnancy/week-by-week/#First-Trimester
- Mayo Clinic. (2024 February 27). *Pregnancy week by week: Pregnancy symptoms*. Mayo Clinic. https://www.mayoclinic.org/healthy-lifestyle/pregnancy-week-by-week/in-depth/pregnancy/art-20047208#:
- Kernodle Clinic. (n.d.). *15 must-ask questions for your first prenatal appointment*. Kernodle Clinic. https://www.kernodle.com/obgyn_blog/15-must-ask-questions-for-your-first-prenatal-appointment/
- Geisinger. (n.d.). *Questions to ask during prenatal appointments*. Geisinger. https://www.geisinger.org/patient-care/conditions-treatments-specialty/questions-to-ask-during-prenatal-appointments
- What to Expect. (2021 August 23). *11 crucial questions every woman needs to ask her OB-GYN during pregnancy*. What to Expect. https://www.whattoexpect.com/wom/pregnancy/11-crucial-questions-every-woman-needs-to-ask-her-ob-gyn-during-pregnancy.aspx
- OB-GYN Westside. (n.d.). *10 questions to ask your OB-GYN at a prenatal visit*. OB-GYN Westside. https://www.obgynwestside.com/blog/10-questions-to-ask-your-obgyn-at-a-prenatal-visit
- Cleveland Clinic. (2022 November 14). *Pregnancy complications*. Cleveland Clinic. https://my.clevelandclinic.org/health/articles/24442-pregnancy-complications
- Johns Hopkins Medicine. (n.d.). *Complications of pregnancy*. Johns Hopkins Medicine. https://www.hopkinsmedicine.org/health/conditions-and-diseases/staying-healthy-during-pregnancy/complications-of-pregnancy
- Johns Hopkins Medicine. (n.d.). *4 common pregnancy complications*. Johns Hopkins Medicine. https://www.hopkinsmedicine.org/health/conditions-and-diseases/staying-healthy-during-pregnancy/4-common-pregnancy-complications
- American Pregnancy Association. (n.d.). *Common pregnancy complications*. American Pregnancy Association. https://americanpregnancy.org/healthy-pregnancy/pregnancy-complications/common-pregnancy-complications/
- Darwin, Z., Galdas, P., Hinchliff, S., Littlewood, E., McMillan, D., McGowan, L., & Gilbody, S. (26 January 2017). *Fathers' views and experiences of their own mental health during pregnancy and the first postnatal year: A qualitative*

interview study of men participating in the UK Born and Bred in Yorkshire (BaBY) cohort. BMC Pregnancy and Childbirth. https://bmcpregnancychildbirth.biomedcentral.com/articles/10.1186/s12884-017-1229-4
- Holding Hope Marriage and Family Therapy. (2024 April 22). *Active listening: A key to deeper intimacy and understanding in your relationship.* Holding Hope Marriage and Family Therapy. https://holdinghopemft.com/active-listening-a-key-to-deeper-intimacy-and-understanding-in-your-relationship/
- Healthline. (2023 October 16). *Pregnancy mood swings.* Healthline. https://www.healthline.com/health/pregnancy/pregnancy-mood-swings
- Waller-Wise R. (2016). *Birth Plans: Encouraging Patient Engagement.* The Journal of perinatal education, 25(4), 215–222. https://doi.org/10.1891/1058-1243.25.4.215
- Raising Children Network. (n.d.). *Healthy relationships with partners during pregnancy.* Raising Children Network. https://raisingchildren.net.au/pregnancy/pregnancy-for-partners/relationships-and-feelings/healthy-relationships-with-partners-pregnancy
- Allen Wastler. (2022 April 11). *A financial guide for parents.* MassMutual. https://blog.massmutual.com/planning/financial-guide-parents
- MassMutual. (2023 July 14). *How to prepare financially for the birth of a child.* MassMutual. https://blog.massmutual.com/planning/new-parent-finances
- The Bump. (2024 February 27). *Checklist: Baby essentials.* The Bump. https://www.thebump.com/a/checklist-baby-essentials
- Pampers. (2023 January 29). *Baby proofing your home.* Pampers. https://www.pampers.com/en-us/baby/parenting-life/article/baby-proofing-your-home
- Forbes. (2024 January 3). *Average childbirth cost in the U.S.* Forbes. https://www.forbes.com/advisor/health-insurance/average-childbirth-cost/
- What to Expect. (2024 March 22). *Best budgeting apps for families.* What to Expect. https://www.whattoexpect.com/family/finances/best-budgeting-apps-for-families
- Bankrate. (2023 January 10). *How to open a 529 college savings plan.* Bankrate. https://www.bankrate.com/investing/how-to-open-529-college-savings-plan/
- Parents. (2023 May 31). *32 ways to save money when you have a baby.* Parents. https://www.parents.com/parenting/money/family-finances/32-ways-to-save-money-when-you-have-a-baby/

- NerdWallet. (2023 December 12). *A new parent's guide to life insurance.* NerdWallet. https://www.nerdwallet.com/article/insurance/a-new-parents-guide-to-life-insurance
- Parents Estate Planning. (n.d.). *Kids protection planning guide.* Parents Estate Planning. https://parentsestateplanning.com/kppguide/
- WebMD. (2023 June 09). *How to create a birth plan.* WebMD. https://www.webmd.com/baby/how-to-create-a-birth-plan
- The Mother Baby Center. (2023 April 28). *C-section vs. vaginal birth.* The Mother Baby Center. https://www.themotherbabycenter.org/blog/2023/04/c-section-vs-vaginal-birth/
- UNICEF. (n.d.). *Skin-to-skin contact.* UNICEF. https://www.unicef.org.uk/babyfriendly/baby-friendly-resources/implementing-standards-resources/skin-to-skin-contact/#:
- Babylist. (2024 July 10). *What to pack in your hospital bag.* Babylist. https://www.babylist.com/hello-baby/what-to-pack-in-your-hospital-bag
- Inspira Health Network. (2023 October 6). *The role of a midwife in maternity care.* Inspira Health Network. https://www.inspirahealthnetwork.org/news/role-midwife-maternity-care
- American Pregnancy Association. (n.d.). *The benefits of midwives.* American Pregnancy Association. https://americanpregnancy.org/healthy-pregnancy/labor-and-birth/midwives/
- Cleveland Clinic. (n.d.). *What is a midwife? When to see one, what to expect.* Cleveland Clinic. https://my.clevelandclinic.org/health/articles/21194-what-is-a-midwife-when-to-see-one-what-to-expect
- American Pregnancy Association. (n.d.). *Having a doula.* American Pregnancy Association. https://americanpregnancy.org/healthy-pregnancy/labor-and-birth/having-a-doula/
- Cleveland Clinic. (n.d.). *Doula.* Cleveland Clinic. https://my.clevelandclinic.org/health/articles/22620-doula
- Reproductivia. (n.d.). *The role of doulas during pregnancy and delivery.* Reproductivia. https://reproductivia.com/the-role-of-doulas-during-pregnancy-and-delivery/
- Cleveland Clinic. (n.d.). *Pregnancy complications.* Cleveland Clinic. https://my.clevelandclinic.org/health/articles/9431-pregnancy-complications
- Pregnancy Birth Baby. (n.d.). *What does an obstetrician do?.* Pregnancy Birth Baby. https://www.pregnancybirthbaby.org.au/the-role-of-your-obstetrician
- CareerExplorer. (n.d.). *What is an Obstetrician?.* CareerExplorer. https://www.careerexplorer.com/careers/obstetrician/

REFERENCES 165

- Gynaecologist.org.uk. (n.d.). *Obstetrics: Procedures and complications in pregnancy.* Gynaecologist.org.uk. https://www.gynaecologist.org.uk/obstetrics-procedures-complications-pregnancy
- MSD Manuals. (2024 March). *Analgesia and Anesthesia for Labor and Delivery.* MSD Manuals. https://www.msdmanuals.com/professional/gynecology-and-obstetrics/labor-and-delivery/analgesia-and-anesthesia-for-labor-and-delivery
- American Society of Anesthesiologists. (2016). *Practice guidelines for obstetric anesthesia.* American Society of Anesthesiologists. https://www.asahq.org/~/media/sites/asahq/files/public/resources/standards-guidelines/practice-guidelines-for-obstetric-anesthesia.pdf
- Cleveland Clinic. (n.d.). *Anesthesiologist.* Cleveland Clinic. https://my.clevelandclinic.org/health/articles/21198-anesthesiologist
- Oxford University Press. (2017 April). *Chapter in book.* Oxford University Press. https://academic.oup.com/book/30062/chapter/256319690
- NurseJournal.org. (2024 June 26). *Labor and delivery nurse.* NurseJournal.org. https://nursejournal.org/careers/labor-and-delivery-nurse/
- Carrying To Term. (n.d.). *The role of a labor and delivery nurse and how they can help.* Carrying To Term. https://carryingtoterm.org/the-role-of-a-labor-and-delivery-nurse-and-how-they-can-help/
- What to Expect. (2022 August 12). *Childproofing basics.* What to Expect. https://www.whattoexpect.com/nursery-decorating/childproofing-basics.aspx
- Babyation. (n.d.). *5 design principles for a peaceful nursery.* Babyation. https://blog.babyation.com/5-design-principles-peaceful-nursery/
- PopSugar. (2023 December 5). *Best baby gear.* PopSugar. https://www.popsugar.com/family/best-baby-gear-45632058
- Lancaster General Health. (n.d.). *Car seat safety: Choosing an infant car seat.* Lancaster General Health. https://www.lancastergeneralhealth.org/health-hub-home/motherhood/your-pregnancy/car-seat-safety-choosing-an-infant-car-seat
- Sharp Health News. (2023 November 15). *Used baby gear: Is it safe?.* Sharp Health News. https://www.sharp.com/health-news/used-baby-gear-is-it-safe#:
- Mercy. (n.d.). *A dad's role in labor and delivery.* Mercy. https://www.mercy.net/service/childbirth/a-dads-role-in-labor-and-delivery/
- Mayo Clinic. (2024 July 23). *Stages of labor.* Mayo Clinic. https://www.mayoclinic.org/healthy-lifestyle/labor-and-delivery/in-depth/stages-of-labor/art-20046545

REFERENCES

- BabyCenter. (2021 October 29). *A childbirth cheat sheet for dads-to-be.* BabyCenter. https://www.babycenter.com/pregnancy/relationships/a-childbirth-cheat-sheet-for-dads-to-be_8244
- NCBI. (2024 January 1). *Father involvement in labor and delivery.* NCBI. https://www.ncbi.nlm.nih.gov/pmc/articles/PMC10844877/
- High Speed Daddy. (2019 December 30). *31 first-time dad tips for labor and delivery.* High Speed Daddy. https://highspeeddaddy.com/blogs/hsd-blog/31-first-time-dad-tips-for-labor-delivery
- The Bump. (2023 October 25). *Tips for birth support people.* The Bump. https://www.thebump.com/a/tips-for-birth-support-people
- The Mother Baby Center. (2022 July 20). *Types of birth: Pros and cons of common delivery methods.* The Mother Baby Center. https://www.themotherbabycenter.org/blog/2022/07/types-of-birth-pros-and-cons-of-common-delivery-methods
- NCBI. (2011). *Father involvement in early child care.* NCBI. https://www.ncbi.nlm.nih.gov/pmc/articles/PMC3209754/#:
- HealthyChildren.org. (2020 January 15). *Common Diaper Rashes & Treatments.* HealthyChildren.org. https://www.healthychildren.org/English/ages-stages/baby/diapers-clothing/Pages/Diaper-Rash.aspx
- Babylist. (2023 December 5). *How to Set Up a Diaper Changing Station.* Babylist. https://www.babylist.com/hello-baby/how-to-set-up-diaper-changing-station
- Stanford Children's Health. (n.d.). *Newborn Sleep Patterns.* Stanford Children's Health. https://www.stanfordchildrens.org/en/topic/default?id=newborn-sleep-patterns-90-P02632
- What to Expect. (2022 May 18). *Baby Bedtime Routine.* What to Expect. https://www.whattoexpect.com/first-year/sleep/baby-bedtime-routine/
- Today's Parent. (2024 May 03). *Bathing Your New Baby.* Today's Parent. https://www.todaysparent.com/baby/bathing-your-new-baby/
- Nationwide Children's Hospital. (n.d.). *Bathing Your Baby.* Nationwide Children's Hospital. https://www.nationwidechildrens.org/family-resources-education/health-wellness-and-safety-resources/helping-hands/bathing-your-baby
- What to Expect. (2024 April 19). *Mom's Favorite Bottles.* What to Expect. https://www.whattoexpect.com/baby-products/nursing-feeding/moms-favorite-bottles/
- NCT. (2017 October). *How Can Dads and Partners Support Breastfeeding.* NCT. https://www.nct.org.uk/baby-toddler/feeding/tips-for-dads-and-partners/how-can-dads-and-partners-support-breastfeeding

- CDC. (2024 April 16). *Cleaning, Sanitizing, and Disinfecting in Child Care Settings*. CDC. https://www.cdc.gov/hygiene/childcare/clean-sanitize.html
- NHS. (2023 March 30). *Combining Breast and Bottle*. NHS. https://www.nhs.uk/conditions/baby/breastfeeding-and-bottle-feeding/bottle-feeding/combine-breast-and-bottle/#:
- HealthyChildren.org. (2022 March 21). *How to Calm a Fussy Baby*. HealthyChildren.org. https://www.healthychildren.org/English/ages-stages/baby/crying-colic/Pages/How-to-Calm-a-Fussy-Baby.aspx
- Happiest Baby. (n.d.). *The 5 S's for Soothing Babies*. Happiest Baby. https://www.happiestbaby.com/blogs/baby/the-5-s-soothing-babies
- Fatherly. (n.d.). *Soothing Techniques to Calm a Fussy Baby*. Fatherly. https://www.fatherly.com/health-science/soothing-techniques-calm-fussy-baby/
- The Fussy Baby Site. (n.d.). *40 Fussy Baby Soothing Techniques*. The Fussy Baby Site. https://www.thefussybabysite.com/blog/40-fussy-baby-soothing-techniques/
- Cleveland Clinic. (2022 April 12). *Postpartum Depression*. Cleveland Clinic. https://my.clevelandclinic.org/health/diseases/9312-postpartum-depression
- COPE. (n.d.). *Building a Support Network*. COPE. https://www.cope.org.au/new-parents/emotional-health-new-parents/building-a-support-network/
- Johns Hopkins Medicine. (n.d.). *What Really Helps You Bounce Back After Pregnancy*. Johns Hopkins Medicine. https://www.hopkinsmedicine.org/health/wellness-and-prevention/what-really-helps-you-bounce-back-after-pregnancy
- Mrs. Mummy PhD. (2024 September 06). *Dads Should Prioritise Self-Care*. Mrs. Mummy PhD. https://mrsmummyphd.com/dads-should-prioritise-self-care/
- Mental Health America. (n.d.). *Mental Health and New Fathers*. Mental Health America. https://www.mhanational.org/mental-health-and-new-father
- Heads Up Guys. (2021 January 30). *Becoming a Dad: Maintaining Mental Health*. Heads Up Guys. https://headsupguys.org/new-dad-mental-health/
- Psychology Today. (2016 March 22). *The Mental Health of Dads Matters*. Psychology Today. https://www.psychologytoday.com/us/blog/women-s-mental-health-matters/201603/the-mental-health-dads-matters
- Psychology Today. (2021 December 31). *What Postpartum Depression Looks Like in New Dads*. Psychology Today. https://www.psychologytoday.com/us/blog/psychiatry-the-people/202112/what-postpartum-depression-

REFERENCES

looks-in-new-dads
- CDC. (2023 June 06). *Developmental Milestones at 1 Year*. CDC. https://www.cdc.gov/ncbddd/actearly/milestones/milestones-1yr.html
- NICHD. (n.d.). *Tummy Time*. NICHD. https://safetosleep.nichd.nih.gov/reduce-risk/tummy-time#:)
- CDC. (2023, June 27). *When, What, and How to Introduce Solid Foods*. CDC. https://www.cdc.gov/nutrition/infantandtoddlernutrition/foods-and-drinks/when-to-introduce-solid-foods.html
- Help Me Grow Minnesota. (n.d.). *Social Skills in Babies*. Help Me Grow Minnesota. https://helpmegrowmn.org/HMG/HelpfulRes/Articles/socialskillsbabies/index.htm
- CDC. (2024 July 24). *Child and Adolescent Immunization Schedule*. CDC. https://www.cdc.gov/vaccines/schedules/easy-to-read/child-easyread.html
- CDC. (2024 May 08). *Milestones in Child Development*. CDC. https://www.cdc.gov/ncbddd/actearly/milestones/index.html
- The Bump. (2023 September 18). *Checklist: Babyproofing, Part 1*. The Bump. https://www.thebump.com/a/checklist-babyproofing-part-1
- Red Cross. (n.d.). *Child and Baby First Aid*. Red Cross. https://www.redcross.org/take-a-class/first-aid/performing-first-aid/child-baby-first-aid#:
- CDC. (2019 August 01). *Why Vaccinate?*. CDC. https://www.cdc.gov/vaccines/parents/why-vaccinate/index.html
- WHO. (2020 December 08). *How Do Vaccines Work?*. WHO. https://www.who.int/news-room/feature-stories/detail/how-do-vaccines-work
- HealthyChildren.org. (n.d.). *How to Talk to Parents about Vaccines*. HealthyChildren.org. https://www.healthychildren.org/English/safety-prevention/immunizations/Pages/How-to-Talk-to-Parents-about-Vaccines.aspx
- National Vaccine Information Center. (n.d.). *Discussing Vaccine Risks*. NVIC. https://www.nvic.org/Doctors-Corner/Discussing-Vaccine-Risks.aspx
- Children's Hospital of Philadelphia. (n.d.). *Vaccine Education Center*. CHOP. https://www.chop.edu/centers-programs/vaccine-education-center/vaccine-concerns
- Mayo Clinic. (2023 September 22). *Infant Vaccines*. Mayo Clinic. https://www.mayoclinic.org/healthy-lifestyle/infant-and-toddler-health/in-depth/infant-vaccines/art-20048000
- CDC. (2020 July 17). *Vaccine Safety Concerns*. CDC. https://www.cdc.gov/vaccinesafety/concerns/index.html

- FDA. (n.d.). *Vaccine Basics*. FDA. https://www.fda.gov/vaccines-blood-biologics/vaccine-basics
- Nanit. (n.d.). *Why Date Nights are a Must for New Parents*. Nanit. https://www.nanit.com/blogs/parent-confidently/why-date-nights-are-a-must-for-new-parents-11-ideas-to-create-connection-after-baby
- TendTask. (n.d.). *Balancing Parenting and Marriage: Tips for Couples*. TendTask. https://tendtask.com/journal/balancing-parenting-and-marriage-tips-for-couples/
- UNICEF. (n.d.). *9 Tips for Better Communication*. UNICEF. https://www.unicef.org/parenting/child-care/9-tips-for-better-communication
- Jason Kreidman. (2019 August 8). *How to Change a Diaper - Expert Tips on Changing a Baby | Dad University*. YouTube. http://www.youtube.com/watch?v=CAPjF-RCpro&t=321s
- The Doctors Bjorkman. (2021 June 16). *Pediatrician Tips for Swaddling Baby to Get More Sleep*. YouTube. http://www.youtube.com/watch?v=ayjlY3RnTrE&t=580s
- Nicklaus Children's Hospital. (2019 October 4). *How to perform first aid and CPR on a choking infant / baby?*. YouTube. http://www.youtube.com/watch?v=gHZdBY-CkGw&t=2s